GOD REIGNS IN CHINA

GOD REIGNS IN CHINA

Leslie Lyall

Look among the nations, and see; wonder and be astounded. For I am doing a work in your days that you would not believe if told.

Habakkuk 1:5

HODDER AND STOUGHTON
LONDON SYDNEY AUCKLAND TORONTO
AND
THE OVERSEAS MISSIONARY FELLOWSHIP

British Library Cataloguing in Publication Data

Lyall, Leslie T.
  God reigns in China—(Hodder Christian paperbacks)
  1. China—Church history
  I. Title
  275.1   BR1285

  ISBN 0-340-36199-9

Contents

Acknowledgments

In accumulating the information in this book it is not poss-
ible to give the source of every statement and every detail.
But I gladly acknowledge my indebtedness to the Christian
China Study Group (London) Reports, the Bulletin of the
China Study Project (British Council of Churches) and the
publications of Asian Outreach (Hong Kong), Pray for
China (Christian Communications Ltd, Hong Kong),
Chinese Church Research Centre (Hong Kong), Far East
Broadcasting Company (Hong Kong), Chinese Around the
World, Information Letter of Lutheran World Federation
(Switzerland), *Alive in the Bitter Sea* by Fox Butterfield, *The
Dragon and the Bear* by Philip Short, *Households of God* by
Raymond Fung, God Lives in China (China Bible Fund)
and the Prayer Letters of the China Programme (OMF).

A Note on the Spelling of Chinese Names

The present Chinese Government has rejected the familiar
Wade-Giles romanisation of proper names in favour of a
system of its own. The author has adopted the latter, except
in the case of names universally familiar in the traditional
spelling, such as Peking, Canton, Amoy and Hong Kong.

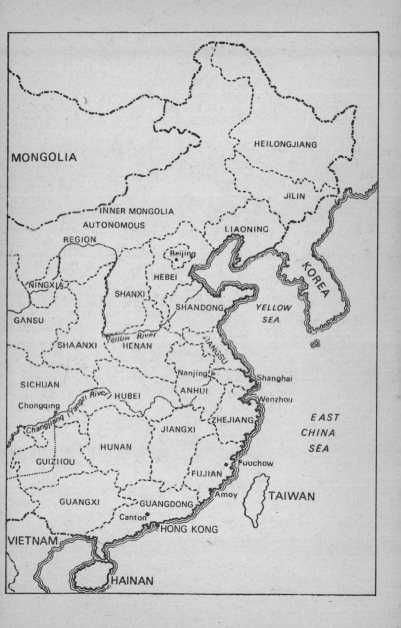

Foreword
by James H. Taylor III

"The trend of a lifetime, not the emotion of a moment is the way in which God's call to China has come to me." Thus wrote Leslie Lyall, a 23-year-old Cambridge graduate, on the eve of his departure for China fifty-five years ago.

God Reigns in China is the rich and rewarding product of that "trend of a lifetime". Leslie Lyall arrived in China in response to the China Inland Mission's appeal for 200 evangelists. The Nationalist army's northern expedition, barely concluded, had brought a deceptive and short-lived tranquillity and unity to the nation. There the author's first inland appointment was to Shanxi Province in north China where, in a nearby village, Hua Guofeng, a lad of ten, was growing up unnoticed. From those early years of pioneer evangelism through the China Inland Mission's and his own "reluctant exodus" from China twenty years later, Leslie Lyall was an active participant in, as well as a perceptive observer of, God's sovereign ordering of events.

This book traces against a clear Biblical and historical background the remarkable movements of God's Spirit in the Chinese Church. Not only is it a moving testimony of the author's own experience in service but it provides invaluable vignettes of many leading Chinese Christians.

The reader who wants to know what God has been doing in China these past thirty years, especially about the unbelievable growth of the Church, will find in the second half of *God Reigns in China* a clear and reliable account. I know of no one who has been a more faithful China-watcher or who has grasped the complexities of the situation more

clearly than Leslie Lyall. The insights he gives into the
nature of the Church and Marxist society, into the development of the house church movement with its strengths and
weaknesses and his objective assessment of the Three-Self
Patriotic Movement are all tremendous contributions to the
concerned Christian's understanding of the Church in China
today.

> *O clap your hands, all peoples;*
> Shout to God with the voice of joy
>
> God reigns over the nations,
> God sits on His holy throne.
> *Psalm 47:1, 8*

James H. Taylor III

Author's Introduction

This book, based on the author's own journals, traces the sovereign hand of God at work in China over the past half-century. Today, the world is witnessing an extraordinary revival of Christianity in the land that only recently worshipped Mao Zedong with intense religious fervour and where the Red Guards attempted to eliminate religion altogether. The current phenomenal growth of the Church in China is, however, no isolated or unrelated occurrence but must be seen as the direct result of the divine activity, both in the political sphere and in the Church, particularly over the past fifty years.

Against the backcloth of China's revolutionary history a drama has been unfolding. First, following the failure of the Nationalist Revolution, there was in 1926 the abortive attempt to unify a country torn asunder by warlords. Then followed a long and bloody civil war during which a Communist remnant, to escape encirclement, made the epic Long March from south China to a new northern redoubt in the mountain caves of Yanan. There the gathering strength of Communist propaganda and military might led to a closing of the ranks between Nationalists and Communists in order to oppose Japanese aggression. Eight years of war were followed by the collapse of the Nationalist government and the establishment of the People's Government of China. Finally, the world witnessed the early successes and subsequent disastrous failures of government under the rule of Mao Zedong. These events have proved to be the crucible in which God has been moulding something new for His glory.

Widespread revival and intensified evangelism in the thirties had prepared the Church for the fiery trials of war. That war had caused an unprecedented movement of population from east to west and so brought the world of learning as never before within the orbit of the Christian fellowship. In the post-war years a powerful spiritual movement affected all China's universities. And yet when Communism triumphed in 1949 the Protestant Church numbered fewer than one million communicant members – a quite insignificant minority in the world's most populous nation. But in spite of the oppression, persecution and intense suffering under Maoist rule, the Church multiplied greatly. And the only possible explanation for this phenomenon is God's sovereign rule in China.

The writer of the second psalm vividly portrays the turmoil of nations in revolution and the secret conspiring for the overthrow of governments. He describes the din of the rioting mobs, and even anticipates the blasphemous effrontery of the Red Guards in Shanghai who displayed a placard on which were written the words "Hang God!" "Why do the nations rage and tumultuously assemble and the people plot in vain?" asks the psalmist. "The rulers take counsel together against the Lord and His anointed saying 'Let us burst their bonds asunder and cast them from us!'" But God's response was to raise Christ from the dead and exalt Him above all authority in heaven and earth and to entrust to Him the dominion of the world. "Ask of Me and I will make the nations your heritage!" was the Father's legacy to His risen Son. Thereafter, Jesus could confidently proclaim: "All power and authority, both in heaven and on earth, is given to Me!" Jesus is King of kings and Lord of lords; and every challenge to His Lordship, whether from China, Russia or the equally godless "free world" is doomed to failure. For "our God reigns" and He reigns in China!

1 A Great Leap of Faith (1929–31)

"God is the King of all the earth; sing praises with a psalm!"

Psalm 47:7

The year was 1929. The ancient pagoda towering over the riverside walled city told us that we had reached our destination. The ship's engines slowed down while the murky, turbulent waters of the mighty Changjiang (Yangzi) River, flowing down from the melting snows of Tibet, surged past its bows. The passengers prepared to disembark in mid-stream and clambered over the side into a barge lashed to the ship. The barge then swung through the swift current to the muddy north bank, where five young men walked the plank above the swirling waters on to dry ground. This was Anqing, capital city of the province of Anhui. All was bustle and din as coolies clamoured and bargained for the opportunity to transport our "pigskin" boxes on carrying-poles to the premises of the language school.

The first experience of walking down a Chinese city street was novel and exciting. The open-fronted shops with their intriguing signs written in mysterious Chinese ideographs, the itinerant food pedlars and barbers each with their distinctive cries, the powerful smell of open drains mingling with the pungent odours of strange spices and the dense crowds of blue-gowned people formed an indelible first impression.

Three days of luxury travel on a Jardine and Matheson river steamer lay behind us. Riverside scenes at Zhenjiang,

Nanjing and Wuhu had been fascinating. The great variety of merchandise unloaded by the coolies to the accompaniment of rhythmic chanting had provided a glimpse of the vast commercial potential of this huge and amazing country and its burgeoning millions. The vessel we had left would sail on to Hankow and Yichang, where smaller vessels would continue the journey to Chongqing through the beautiful gorges and up the fierce rapids where so many small craft have been wrecked. Early missionaries travelling by houseboat had been hauled all the way by trackers. The Yangzi is the broad and swift-flowing river dividing north China from south which, until the Communists came to power, had never been bridged. Today there are splendid bridges at Nanjing, Hankow and Chongqing.

That autumn we five had already voyaged for six weeks from London to Shanghai on board the *Kashima Maru*. We had spent a week at the original, colonial-style Woosung Road headquarters of the China Inland Mission, of which we were the newest recruits. This mission had been founded in 1865 by James Hudson Taylor with the aim of evangelising the vast interior of China. We had received a cordial welcome from D. E. Hoste, the whimsical, godly, prayerful general director, one of a group of prominent sportsmen and army officers known as the "Cambridge Seven" who had arrived in that country in 1885. Hoste had succeeded Hudson Taylor as general director in 1902 and so had already led the Mission for nearly thirty years. Though venerable in appearance – a modern patriarch – Mr Hoste still retained his upright, military bearing.

In 1926 China was emerging from a deep crisis. The shooting of a Communist student agitator by a British policeman in Shanghai's British Concession in May of the previous year had been the spark to the tinder-box, and a resounding explosion had followed. The first Communist-inspired anti-foreign movement had swept through the country, causing missionaries to be hastily recalled to the safety of the coastal ports. Nearly 2,000 of them, believing that missionary work was already doomed, had left China never to return. It had also been a time of deep trouble for the Christian churches, as Communist propaganda identified them with foreign imperialism and their members were scornfully dubbed "running dogs of the imperialists". Missionaries of the China Inland Mission (CIM) spent two years at the coast under very crowded conditions and facing an uncertain future, but during that time they reconsidered their basic policies while waiting hopefully and patiently for the doors to inland China to reopen.

In 1926 the southern Nationalists in Canton under General Chiang Kai-shek decided that the time had come to unify a deeply divided nation. Nationalist and Communist forces had then marched north together and quickly occupied the Yangzi cities. But, as Mao Zedong and the Communists parted company with the Nationalists, a long and devastating civil war began. Chiang Kai-shek's armies immediately swung east to secure the strategic city of Shanghai, where many Communist sympathisers were executed. Alarmed at the threat to British commercial interests, the British Government dispatched an expeditionary force to Shanghai to protect the rich international settlements. There refugee missionaries found welcome opportunities for a Christian witness among British servicemen.

The worst of the crisis was over by 1928, and the foreign consuls gave permission for missionaries to return to their stations. CIM leaders had meanwhile sensed the urgency to reach out to the many unevangelised regions and peoples of China. In 1929, therefore, D. E. Hoste issued his historic appeal for 200 evangelists to reach China within two years. In view of the prevailing chaos the timing of the appeal, humanly speaking, could not have been less opportune. But Hoste was a modern Caleb: no mountain was insuperable for this man of faith, and it was he who took this "great leap forward".

The five young men arriving at Anqing to attend the language school were the "vanguard" of these reinforcements. Within days they were joined by Americans, Canadians, Australians, New Zealanders, Swiss, Germans

and Swedes – a wonderfully varied and happy mix of
nationalities, temperaments and accents – to commence the
awesome study of the Chinese language. Down river at
Yangzhou an international group of ladies were likewise
starting six months of intensive language study. Those were
the days when both commercial firms and missionary
societies normally required their members to remain un-
married for at least two years in order to give them the
opportunity to devote themselves single-mindedly to the
study of Chinese and adaptation to Chinese culture. The
language schools were therefore segregated! The regulations
undoubtedly had their advantages.

The men were greatly privileged in having a unique
Chinese teacher named Yen who was also an accomplished
artist. While knowing no English, he had the great gift of
mime and humour; and he taught us, word by word, line
upon line, by the direct method. Fifty years later it is easy
to recall the excitement and the fun of taking our first
steps in Chinese. Yen was assisted by several ageing and
bewhiskered "scholars" who, sipping their green tea, would
listen sleepily to their pupils spelling out the Gospel of John
word by word. An unorthodox variety of basketball played
every afternoon had been an opportunity to let off steam
and to take our much-needed exercise.

To the south of us, just across the Yangzi River, in the
province of Jiangxi, the civil war between the Nationalists
and the Communist armies was raging. Three Finnish lady
missionaries had been murdered by Communist soldiers
earlier in the year, and another young couple, also members
of the Two Hundred, would be beheaded two years later
not far away. Other missionaries in different parts of China
had either been held for ransom or executed by the Communists as "imperialists". Before many weeks of language study
were past the peace of our city was rudely disturbed by an
attempted revolt of the local garrison. The revolt was
crushed, but from then on we were confined to the comparative safety of the language school premises. No one could
any longer harbour illusions about the battle we were facing.

At the end of six months a mission director arrived from Shanghai to hold personal interviews with each student and to disclose to which province he or she had been "designated". Then, with a mere smattering of the language, these youthful pioneers dispersed to all parts of China to join in the "forward movement". Our group was followed by other groups until the full Two Hundred were positioned to carry out the planned advance.

Perhaps the most dramatic move was to post seven men, including a doctor, to Chinese Turkestan (Xinjiang Province) in Central Asia. They had made the hazardous journey by truck across north China and the Gobi Desert to Urumqi (Tihwa), the provincial capital. Their leader was George Hunter OBE, the veteran who had been the lone missionary representative in that region since 1908, long before even Percy Mather and Mildred Cable and her two companions (popularly known as "the Trio") had undertaken their epic travels distributing the Scriptures throughout the oases of that vast area. The men soon found themselves in the midst of a local civil war and a typhus epidemic. The young doctor, after less than two years in China, contracted the disease from his soldier patients and died; whereupon his younger brother in Scotland immediately volunteered to fill his place. Over fifty years later and thirty years after the Communist Revolution, grateful local Christians continued to care lovingly for the doctor's grave and its headstone. And in contrast to that year of 1934 there is, half a century later, a large, thriving church in Urumqi and there are thousands of Christians in the province, showing that the labour and sacrifice of the pioneers were not in vain.

The appeal for the Two Hundred was bold and imaginative, coming as it did at a very dark moment in China's modern history. It certainly imparted a fresh impetus to the work of the China Inland Mission and aroused world-wide interest. God reigns, and in His sovereign foreknowledge of China's future history He found in D. E. Hoste a man after His own heart to whom He could reveal His will. At just the right moment He injected into the missionary force in

China a band of men and women whose hearts He had touched, and a powerful offensive was launched against Satan's strongholds. Through these men and women thousands of Chinese would be introduced to the Saviour, churches would be planted in all parts of China, and many future Christian leaders would be instructed in the Scriptures and trained for their tasks. The Two Hundred would soon be proclaiming Christ to the many tribes among the mountains of the south-west, to the Tibetans along the lofty borders of that semi-closed land, to the people inhabiting the oases of Turkestan in Central Asia, to the Mongols of the northern steppes and to the fierce Muslims of the north and south-west. They would also minister to the sick in a score of hospitals and break new ground in reaching out to China's children and youth. Some of them would eventually become deeply involved in fruitful work among university students; while others would teach in Christian high schools, Bible schools and theological colleges. Scholars would devote themselves to translating the Scriptures into Tibetan, Mongolian and tribal languages, and missionary women would contribute greatly to the extension of literacy. Even where there was no immediate response, the imperishable seed of God's Word would be sown in the soil of China to germinate and, fifty years on, to yield an abundant harvest. How very different the church situation might have been today but for that great leap of faith and the sovereign act of God in calling out the Two Hundred!

2 Cradle of Chinese Civilisation
(1870—1900)

"The Lord reigns! Thy throne is established from
of old;
Thou art from everlasting!"

Psalm 93:1, 2

It was early spring when I first arrived in the province of
Shanxi. After serving for a year as a supply teacher in the
Chefoo school for missionaries' children on the coast of
Shandong Province, I had travelled inland, stopping long
enough in Peking to fall in love with that historic and
beautiful old capital. Now, too, began a love affair with
the rugged northern province of Shanxi. The ever-present
mountains and the golden landscape with its deep gullies
worn by centuries of wheeled traffic remain etched on the
memory. The constant sunshine and cloudless blue skies in
summer and winter alike were interrupted only by the
monsoon storms of July and August. The blaze of fruit
blossom and the young wheat in spring and the high stands
of maize and sorghum millet in autumn are unforgettable
scenes. Memory recalls the caravans of camels with their
loads of cotton, the pack mules and their muleteers, the
mule carts for merchandise and the covered Peking carts for
travellers. The ancient walled cities dating back to the
days of Abraham, entered through massive gates beneath
picturesque towers and with their fascinating markets and
fairs, never lost their interest. And who of us can forget the

lovely cool summer resort in the hills where water-mills had been transformed into holiday residences and flowers bloomed in abundance? It was there that some of us met our future life partners.

At the end of the journey from Peking I stepped from the train on to the soil of Shanxi to continue the journey south along the rutted one and only motor road in an old Morris car driven by a senior missionary. Having at last reached my appointed field of service, I felt supremely happy. Crawling from walled city to walled city at about twenty miles an hour between dry, dusty fields, we suddenly found ourselves in the midst of great fertility, running streams and lush vegetation. This was the district of Hongdong and Dzaocheng, the two counties fortunate enough to be irrigated from springs which gush out perennially from beneath a rocky eminence. A monastery containing one of China's most ancient collections of Buddhist classics stands on the rock. Hongdong was to be my first inland station. There I took up residence in the splendid premises of the Hoste Memorial School, with young life all around me. Once a year the whole school attended the fair at the spring, where staff and boys witnessed to the crowds, speaking of the Living Water which Christ promises to all who are thirsty. Dzaocheng, incidentally, was the native city of Hua Guofeng, the former Party chairman and premier of China. Did he, I wonder, as a young man attending the fair, ever listen to this message?

Hongdong was the administrative centre for the China Inland Mission in Shanxi. Besides the Hoste Schools on a hill outside there was in the city itself a Bible institute for the training of evangelists and church leaders. Further south, in Linfen, a hospital served the medical needs of the district, and a second hospital in Luan or Changzhi served the east of the province. Of the thirty-eight counties for which the CIM was responsible, missionaries resided in only about twelve.

Shanxi is enfolded in a great bend of the Yellow River as it flows from Tibet towards the sea. This province, whose name means "west of the mountains", is as large as England

and both fertile and beautiful. Prevailing winds blowing from the Gobi Desert have over the centuries deposited thick layers of golden dust or loess over the whole region. The Yellow River carries such a heavy load of this silt that it has built up its bed above the level of the surrounding plains; by periodically bursting its banks at flood time it has frequently caused widespread devastation and heavy loss of life, so earning the name of "China's sorrow". In almost regular cycles the late summer monsoon rains fail and famine results. The great famine of 1875 in which 75% of the population of seventy million people died of starvation, called world-wide attention to this "cradle of Chinese civilisation".

Chinese history seems to have begun in this province, for it was here that the Five Rulers of the legendary period held court. They included the emperors Yao and Shun (2300 BC), whose reigns have always been regarded as China's golden age, the traditional Chinese, unlike the Communists, looking back to the past rather than forward to the future for their utopia. In the north of the province the Mountains of the Five Peaks (Wu Tai Shan) are one of the oldest and most notable centres of Buddhist pilgrimage, where hundreds of splendid temples cluster amid the beautiful alpine ranges; they once attracted thousands of pilgrims from Tibet, Mongolia and Manchuria to the annual festival.

Shanxi is immensely rich in coal deposits, but these were scarcely exploited until after the Communist Revolution, one reason being the almost total lack of railways and even roads. The first north-south narrow-gauge railway in the province was not constructed until the 1930s, before which a single unmetalled road, often impassable in the rainy season, had provided a very limited bus service. In most parts of the province travel and transport were still by the age-old methods of pack mule and camel caravan. In the 1930s we would pass men with bare oil lamps attached to their foreheads digging coal from shallow holes in the hills and loading it on to carts. Today the whole lovely countryside of yesterday has become a vast industrial coalfield served by a new rail network.

This province was to become the scene of a divine activity perhaps unique in the history of the Chinese Church, a kind of experimental testing ground for purely indigenous evangelism, for sheer survival in a terrible holocaust, for the outworking of spiritual renewal and the emergence of Chinese leadership, all of which would prove to be of great significance in the experience of the Church under Communism. A sovereign God who knew the future was already ensuring not only the survival but the phenomenal growth of His Church.

Protestant missionaries first visited Shanxi in 1866; but it was in 1877, following the disastrous famine, that representatives of several missions, including Hudson Taylor's wife, went there to engage in famine relief work. That same year David Hill of the Wesleyan Mission in Hankow also visited the province and devised a way of reaching the scholars sitting for the annual examination with the gospel. Hill distributed notices advertising an essay competition outside the examination hall in Taiyuan, the provincial capital. A Confucian scholar by the name of Hsi, in spite of his anti-foreign prejudices and attracted by the money prizes offered, received the Christian treatises which accompanied the competition notices; these had to be read before writing the essays. Of the 120 entries submitted, Hsi's won three of the four prizes; but, more important, the truth of the gospel gripped his heart and mind, and in 1879 Hill led him to saving faith in Christ. Hsi immediately sought deliverance from his opium addiction and, after studying the Bible assiduously for several years, set out on a remarkable missionary career. Pastor Hsi Shengmo (his name, adopted at his baptism, means "conqueror of demons") gathered his own following of disciples and placed them in charge of the churches which he proceeded to establish, one by one, in southern Shanxi. Since opium-smoking was such a universal curse, he combined setting up "opium refuges" with his evangelism and also gained a reputation for the exorcism of evil spirits; he established additional opium refuges in the neighbouring provinces of Shaanxi, Henan and Hebei. It is therefore noteworthy that the most effective early evangelism and church-planting in north China was the work not of foreign missionaries but of a group of Chinese evangelists led by a Confucian scholar. In the 1980s, long after the last missionaries had left China in 1951, history would repeat itself and Chinese missionaries alone would accept the challenge of their nation's evangelisation.

But in 1884 missionary assistance for Pastor Hsi was on the way. The "Cambridge Seven", which included the stroke of the Cambridge boat, the captain of the Cambridge cricket eleven and a test match player plus several officers from élite regiments, had responded to God's call to go to China as missionaries. They had been a sensational attraction when addressing large audiences throughout the United Kingdom prior to sailing for the Far East. On reaching China in 1885 five of the seven were posted to Shanxi, where D. E. Hoste became a close friend and colleague of Pastor Hsi until the latter's death in 1896; while C. T. Studd, the cricketer, and Stanley Smith, the Cambridge stroke, pioneered the work in east Shanxi. (Sixty years later, my wife and I were living in the very house which they had rented and where "Algie" Smith, son of Stanley and co-founder of the Ruanda Medical Mission, had been born.) W. C. Cassels and Montague Beauchamp were soon transferred to Sichuan, where Cassels was later to become the first Anglican bishop. Stanley Smith eventually resigned from the China Inland Mission to found his own small mission (to which Gladys Aylward would one day be attached); and Studd, too, after being invalided home, founded his own mission in Central Africa, the Heart of Africa Mission or the Worldwide Evangelistic Crusade.

In 1883 Timothy Richard of the English Baptist Mission commenced educational and literature work in Taiyuan, and Dr Harold Schofield of the China Inland Mission opened a hospital there. The American Board Mission (Congregational) also set up extensive educational work south of the capital before 1900. But when the Boxer storm broke that year, the Chinese Church was still in its infancy. The order from the Empress Dowager in Peking to the "Boxers" ("Righteous Fist Society") to kill all missionaries and their Chinese converts was countermanded by some provincial governors, but not by the governor of Shanxi; consequently, that province suffered more than any other in the Boxer massacres. In Shanxi alone, 159 missionaries and children died, the bloodiest carnage taking place in Taiyuan. Some were beaten to death; others stoned, hacked to pieces or burned alive in their own homes. Most were beheaded and, in accordance with Chinese tradition, their heads were displayed in cages on the city walls. Many young Chinese converts or their loved ones lost their lives, some having their eyes gouged out or their ears and lips cut off. One pastor who, after being tied to a pillar, spent the night preaching to the bystanders, had his heart torn out by an angry mob. A woman teacher who refused to recant had her feet chopped off before being killed with a sword, while her companion was burnt alive. But this first violent attempt to destroy Christianity by force failed completely, as two later attempts in 1926 and 1966 by the Communists would also fail; indeed, within six years of the massacres the decimated church in Shanxi had more than doubled in number.

Thirty years after the tragedy of 1900, while visiting remote mountain churches, we arrived at a small city where, to our surprise because it was a weekday, we saw Christians coming out of their chapel. We discovered that the leader had been adjudicating between Christians in a case which they would normally have taken to the mandarin for judgment; but here the church was abiding by St Paul's instructions to the Corinthian church. Mr Hu, the leader, had as a young believer in 1900 seen his children killed and his pregnant wife slashed by Boxer swords. As soon as the violence of that terrible event had subsided, the victims had been confronted in court by their attackers with a view to securing justice.

"How should this man who murdered your children be punished?" the judge had asked "old Hu", who had hardly known what to answer and had pleaded for time to consider the matter. Being illiterate, he had asked someone to read to him the Sermon on the Mount; and there he had found his answer and returned to the court. "Set him free! I forgive him!" was Hu's reply to the judge's repeated question. The court had been astounded and had tried to press on him a large sum of indemnity money provided by the government. Hu had reluctantly accepted this and then, poor as he himself was, had proceeded to distribute it to other destitute people in the city. It is not surprising that such a man should have become the leader of the local Christians who, as well as teaching them the Word of God, could even be entrusted with deciding their legal disputes. The Boxer massacre had brought out the very best in Chinese Christians, as suffering under the Communist regime would again do sixty years on. After the Communist victory in 1949, many more Shanxi Christians were martyred and all the churches closed. The Chinese Church has from the beginning been a martyr Church, and predominantly so in Shanxi.

The tragic events of 1900 were still fresh in the memories of many believers thirty years later; but Christians, far from being fearful or reluctant believers, were filled with zeal and love for Christ. As peasant farmers they had to wrest a precarious living from the soil. Most were poor and often illiterate, and yet almost all the churches conducted their own primary schools and helped to support an evangelist or a pastor. Like the churches of Macedonia, "their extreme poverty overflowed in a wealth of liberality".

We of the new generation of missionaries often wrestled with the dire social problems all around us, for we lived in ease and affluence compared with the average Chinese. This affected our relationships with the Chinese in mission employ, whose wages were a mere pittance compared with our own allowances. Considering the prevailing poverty, Chinese Christians found it hard to accept our new policy of reducing financial subsidies to the churches and insisting on their "self-support"; a number of well-trained and able pastors and evangelists consequently left the province to seek employment with other missions which still paid generous salaries to their employees. One of my Chinese language teachers was attracted by Communism, and his arguments in favour of greater equality and the sharing of material things were hard to dismiss. We newcomers often felt guilty and embarrassed, but at the time there seemed to be nothing that we could do.

The "three-self" slogan ("self-supporting, self-governing, self-propagating") had originally been coined in 1851 by Henry Venn, founder of the Church Missionary Society. In the first instance it had been merely a pragmatic policy dictated by circumstances, without any claim to a Biblical basis. Again, in 1928, it was the rise of Communism which forced missions to adopt the "three-self" policy as essential if the Church was to stand on its own feet in the future. But as a policy without a clear Biblical basis it was always an uncertain guide, and it was sometimes rigidly and harshly applied. Missionaries eventually came to see that this rule, like the law of the sabbath, had been made for man's well-being and not for his slavish observance. Moreover, as missionaries left China to work in other East Asian lands, a growing appreciation of the doctrine of the Body of Christ, in which the strong help the weak, the rich the poor and within whose ranks there is no room for "selfhood", diminished the "three-self" emphasis. While the general principle continued to be a rough guide-line to encourage churches to become autonomous, compromises and modifications dictated by national and cultural situations had to be made. The "three-self" law smacked too much of legalism. In practice it provoked immediate hostility in the years after 1928, when the withholding of financial aid was seen by Chinese Christians as an act of betrayal on the part of the missionary societies towards their spiritual children and as a cruel imposition on churches whose members were, for the most part, living in poverty. There was also more than a breath of suspicion: why, it was asked, were the missionaries withholding money contributed by their supporters for the Chinese churches? The new policy had been a bitter pill for such churches to swallow; but after early resistance and thanks to patient explanation it is probable that the thirty-eight counties of Shanxi for which the China Inland Mission was responsible made more progress towards the goal of a healthy autonomy than churches anywhere else in China. This was due not so much to the success of the policy as to the fact that God reigns and often overrules human mistakes and shortcomings for His own glory. The real reasons for the progress made towards an independent church were first spiritual revival and second godly, gifted Chinese leadership; for when God breaks through in revival He changes even the most unpromising situations, and when He raises up men of spiritual authority and vision the Church takes on a new lease of life.

3 The Quickening Spirit (1921–36)

> "Thine, O Lord, is the greatness, and the power,
> and the glory, and the victory, and the majesty . . .
> Thine is the Kingdom and Thou art exalted as
> head above all."
>
> *1 Chronicles 29:11*

In the years before 1900, missionary work all over China had been very hard going. The strong and often violent anti-foreign feeling resulting from what Dr Sun Yat-sen, in his *Three People's Principles* called the "unequal treaties" of 1842 and 1860 – unequal because they were imposed on a reluctant China – militated against any general welcome for the "foreign religion" which had arrived with the British opium traders and merchants and their gunboat protectors. But the first year of the new century proved to be something of a watershed. The refusal by the China Inland Mission to accept from the Chinese Government the proffered indemnity money for the heavy loss of life and damage to property it had suffered in the Boxer uprising made a profound impression on the churches and on officialdom alike. Suddenly, people wanted to become Christians and the number of baptisms increased dramatically. There followed the years of the first National Revolution, a changed emphasis in some missionary quarters on education as the surest way to win over the educated classes, the First World War, and the subsequent emergence of the Chinese Communist Party. Was the Christian Church strong enough to face this new revolutionary situation?

Miss Marie Monsen of Norway thought not. After some years of experience in China in the early 1920s she had reached the conclusion that many church members had no experience of new life in Christ. It appeared that the acceptance of "converts" into the Church twenty years earlier had been too lax. There had been plenty of preaching about the folly of idolatry and the need to turn to the true and living God, but too little about repentance for one's sin and the necessity for the new birth, so that even deacons, elders and pastors had remained unregenerate. Miss Monsen, therefore, with a clear commission from God, travelled widely, exposing sin in the churches in unvarnished terms and calling for a thorough repentance as the essential condition for a rebirth of the Spirit. At the end of every meeting she would stand at the door of the church challenging each departing worshipper, including the pastor and the church leaders, with the question "Are *you* born again?" Some people would run a mile rather than hear this too-personal question put to them! Yet Miss Monsen's ministry in the power of the Spirit started a cleansing, renewing movement in the Chinese Church – and she was not alone.

In 1926 the Bethel Mission of Shanghai invited Mr Paget Wilkes of the Japan Evangelistic Band to speak at its annual convention, the spiritual outcome of which was to be incalculable. A number of young men and women had heart-searching dealings with God as they sought holiness of life, and among them were four or five who caught the vision of their nation's need and indeed of the need of the whole world. Their leader was a junior Post Office official called Andrew Gih, and they proceeded to form themselves into the Worldwide Bethel Evangelistic Band. Following successful revival meetings in Shanghai and other coastal cities, the Band moved into the inland provinces and cities preaching repentance, the new birth, holiness and the fullness of the Spirit. Several of its members were musical, so music and new choruses became a feature of their campaigns. Everywhere they went they urged revived churches to organise their preaching bands and to move out in aggressive evangelism; wherever they went, God worked in power. The churches had never known anything to compare with the enthusiasm, the originality and the clarity with which the message was now coming over from their own native preachers. And as tears of repentance flowed and Christians earnestly sought the infilling of the Spirit, church after church experienced a true reviving accompanied by a new outreach in evangelism.

As the Chinese New Year 1932 dawned, the streets of Huoxian, the city where Miss Mildred Cable and her two companions had once worked, were aglow with the fresh red paper scrolls pasted on every door. On New Year's Eve in every home the kitchen god, witness of so much wrong, had his lips sealed with honey and was sent back to heaven in flames pledged to report no evil. New Year was also the season of obligatory ancestor worship and temple visits, while outside every dwelling joss-sticks were burnt to ward off evil spirits. Normal life came to a standstill for about two weeks, the only general holiday of the year when every family aimed to be reunited. Shanxi men were the nation's bankers and so were scattered throughout every province, but they would all come home for the festivities: the eating, the drinking and the greeting of the New Year with fire-crackers. Courtesy calls on relatives and friends, with appropriate gifts, would follow. Christians customarily used this season as an opportunity for village evangelism.

On New Year's Eve all long-distance bus services passing through Huoxian came to a halt to allow drivers and conductors to celebrate. The luckless passengers had to find accommodation in the city inns for a day or two. Among the passengers that year, on his way to visit his fiancée, was one of the Two Hundred "vanguard" who, impatient as he was, had to be my guest. Because we were very different in temperament there had always been an awkward relationship between the two of us, but at the recent revival meetings held by the Bethel Band in neighbouring Hongdong we had witnessed a powerful work of the Holy Spirit, and God had also searched our own hearts. Now, as in His providence

God brought this old friend so unexpectedly to spend the New Year with me, our hearts were already prepared. We were soon putting right what had been amiss in our relationship; and that New Year's Eve, in my tiny room with its stone floor and paper windows, we found such freedom and fellowship in praise and prayer that the hours slipped by unnoticed. Getting right with God and with one another had been the key – as it always is – to a gracious visitation of the Holy Spirit, and this had already begun in Shanxi.

Meanwhile in the USA, a brilliant young Chinese scientist had gained the highest academic awards and could have held the chair of chemistry at any university he chose; but before leaving America to return to his homeland this man, Dr John Sung, had a profound spiritual experience which changed the direction of his life and led him to give himself and his rich talents to God for the salvation of his people. Forgoing the prospects of wealth and fame, he joined Andrew Gih's Bethel Band, which consequently became even more dynamic in its ministry. None of us who were present when John Sung visited Hongdong with the Band in 1933 can forget the spiritual power which accompanied his often dramatic preaching: missionaries and Chinese alike found themselves kneeling together in humble repentance for sin and spiritual failure and seeking God's fullness of blessing. Before the outbreak of war with Japan in 1937 Sung travelled to Taiwan, Java, Singapore, Malaysia, Burma and Thailand, speaking at evangelistic and revival meetings and holding intensive Bible teaching courses. When, twenty years later, I travelled through these same countries, it was evident that almost all the truly spiritual leaders there were people who had come into a living experience of Christ as a result of John Sung's ministry. In his comparatively short life he had left behind a profound and lasting impression on the churches everywhere in Asia, and long after his death in 1944 Christians still remembered him with both awe and affection. He had been a true John the Baptist preparing the way of the Lord.[1]

But other master builders of the Chinese Church must

also be honoured. In Peking, God raised up a remarkable man to proclaim the same evangelical message. Mr Wang Mingdao was of humble origin and had attended neither university nor Bible college; nor had he studied abroad as so many bright young men of his generation had been able to do. But he was taught of God and deeply versed in the Scriptures, had an eloquent tongue and was able to hold audiences all over China with his expositions of Bible truth. He also possessed a fluent pen, and his quarterly magazine teaching the great foundation truths of the faith enjoyed a wide circulation. Mr Wang did not start a movement, as some of his contemporaries had done, but remained pastor of the Christian Tabernacle, an independent congregation in Peking where innumerable folk, young and old, came to faith in Christ. Applicants for membership were very carefully screened as to the genuineness of their spiritual experience before being accepted for baptism.

It was in Shanghai that Watchman Nee, the other outstanding personality among China's evangelical leaders, established his work in 1928. While a young man in his native Fuzhou he was introduced to the writings of Andrew Murray, Mrs Penn Lewis, D. M. Panton and Samuel Govett, a former Anglican minister, by Miss Margaret Barber, a missionary who had herself left the Church of England to become independent. Nee and a few companions, including Leyland Wang, an ex-naval officer, began to meet in a simple fellowship. On moving to Shanghai in 1921 he met with a few other like-minded friends for Bible study and the "breaking of bread", and out of this small beginning there grew up what was possibly the most influential spiritual movement in China in modern times. The heart of this movement had been the Assembly in Shanghai, but, as with Wang Mingdao, Watchman Nee's published sermons, addresses and Bible expositions enjoyed a very wide circulation. Influenced both by Britain's Exclusive Brethren and by the teachings of Austin Sparks at the Fellowship Centre in Honor Oak, South London, some aspects of Watchman Nee's teaching bordered on sinless perfection. He also insisted on the autonomy of the local church and denounced what he saw as the sins of denominationalism. *Rethinking our Missions* was a Watchman Nee best-seller which rocked foreign missionary societies by its forthright attack on them and their policies. But Nee was an all-round, persuasive exponent of Scripture, and in his assemblies there was a warmth of fellowship and a unique spirituality which held a strong attraction for Western admirers, some of whom left their societies to join them, and more especially for the better-educated Chinese of the cities. Unlike Wang Ming-dao, Nee started an independent movement which induced many churches founded by foreign missions to transfer their allegiance to him. He had a scheme for the intensive training of leaders in the local churches which was excellent and seemed to promote a spirituality deeper than that encouraged by the teaching of the missionaries. He also entered the commercial world of the manufacturing industry with the aim of providing employment for Christian people; a venture which was in the end to get him into trouble with the Communist authorities.

Mention should also be made of other indigenous movements, Pentecostal in origin and character, which contributed to the building of strong, durable indigenous congregations. In 1917 Paul Wei had started a breakaway denomination called the True Jesus Church which grew to large proportions, especially in Fuzhou and Taiwan. The Jesus Family, started in 1926, was an experiment in communal living – almost an attempt to pre-empt Communism itself – which interested the Communists for a while before 1952, when they dissolved the organisation. But both these movements and the Spiritual Gifts Society indulged in a variety of extremes and spiritual counterfeits, sometimes laying aside Scripture in favour of direct "revelation" said to be from the Holy Spirit; at one period they would countenance nothing but the loud unison praying which was a feature of the revival movement everywhere, with individual praying almost excluded. The Jesus Family, in some areas, even conducted lawsuits in attempts to obtain possession of foreign mission property.

There is no doubt that all these indigenous movements were strongly influenced by the spirit of nationalism and a desire to be seen as dissociated from foreign mission agencies. An "independent church movement" had been started as early as 1911, and by separating themselves the independent churches hoped to avoid the stigma of being regarded as disciples of a "foreign" religion. At the same time, there is no doubt that God in His sovereign wisdom had raised up these leaders, as once He had raised up Esther "for such a time as this", to prepare His Church for the severe trials that lay ahead, first during the war with Japan and then in the coming of Communism. Without them the Church might never have survived, and they were undoubtedly the forerunners of the household churches which are multiplying so rapidly today. Even before 1949, the year of the Communist victory, family gatherings, as in New Testament times, existed in their thousands all over China.

Among the Shanxi missionaries there was one Scottish lady with a burden for revival. This was Elizabeth Fischbacher, who, hearing of what God had been doing in Shandong among the missionaries and the churches of the Southern Baptist Mission, went there to investigate for herself. She returned full of what she had witnessed of revival and began to share her burden with her fellow missionaries, the churches and the Bible institute students, with the result that many experienced personal reconciliations, a deeper repentance and a hunger for the Spirit's fullness. A "release of the Spirit" led to new joy and freedom in fellowship, and our weekly station prayer meetings in Hongdong knew a liberty which led to their being extended far beyond the normal one-hour limit. Mutual confession of the sins of criticism, jealousy and lack of love punctuated our prayers as a yearning was expressed for the Spirit's fullness to energise our service for God. One and another experienced individual crises, and a few spoke in tongues, while yet others amongst us were content to claim the fullness by faith, without demanding any external manifestation. Thus the subject of "gifts of the Spirit" was a live issue long before the arrival of the contemporary charismatic movement. As the issue was discussed and prayed about it was noted that St Peter in his epistles never once refers to his own Pentecostal experience, nor does he advocate such an experience for his readers. And St Paul, once he had dealt, at an early stage in Church history, with the abuses of tongues-speaking among the unspiritual Christians at Corinth, never again in the last eleven years of his life made any further reference to the subject in his subsequent letters. Even in the prison epistles, usually regarded as containing the deepest teaching about the Church and the inner life, there is no reference to "tongues", and there is only one mention of Spirit baptism, in Ephesians 4.3, where it is said to be the experience of all believers. If these matters had been so very important one might have expected St Paul, in his parting instructions to Timothy, his spiritual heir and pastor of the large church of Ephesus, to have included teaching on the subjects of Spirit baptism and tongues-speaking; but no, these topics were not included in his priorities. And therefore, in Shanxi, believers were seeking not some emotional experience but the Lord Himself – not the gifts but the Giver – and they were also cautious to test the spirits.

Every revival in history – and in most of those in the past "charismatic" issues seldom arose – has been beset by satanic opposition. Watchman Nee, who himself knew personal renewal but never spoke in tongues, wrote his most important book, *The Spiritual Man*, to help the Chinese Church to distinguish between those manifestations which were "soulish" or of the flesh and the emotions, those which were directly demonic counterfeits (for Satan is the arch-deceiver) and those which were "spiritual" or clearly of the Holy Spirit. He pleaded for spiritual discernment if the Chinese Church was not to fall into error and chaos – which, alas, in many instances it did.

As the tide of revival throughout Shanxi rose, engulfing Chinese and missionaries alike, a spirit of joy and a mutual fellowship closer than ever before prevailed. Our ministry among both young and old was affected, and the year I spent teaching in the Hoste School was a year to be remembered. My room in the school was often filled with eager, seeking youngsters praising the Lord and praying for themselves and for others. Many found Christ for the first time; while others yielded their lives for God's service. Today, forty-five years on, those boys will be in their sixties and seventies, and one can well imagine that while some may have fallen by the wayside, others are standing firm for Christ among the house churches, never able to forget those glorious times when God was so near and Christ so real.

Perhaps some reports of events in Shanxi reaching the CIM headquarters in Shanghai may have been over-enthusiastic and open to misunderstanding; and not every missionary shared the enthusiasm for what was taking place. So in 1935 J. O. Fraser, "Fraser of Lisuland", was asked to visit the province to meet the missionaries at Yü-tao-ho, our picturesque summer resort.

In Yunnan, through the ministry of a Danish lady evangelist, Anna Christensen, and others, the message of repentance and the new birth was revolutionising the work among the Lisu, many of whom had never before experienced the regenerating work of the Spirit. Fraser told the story of revival among his beloved Lisu, while Frank Houghton, editor of *China's Millions* and a future bishop, who was then on a visit to China shared the Bible ministry with him. If there had been any doubts or misgivings in either of their minds about possible excesses these were soon swept away, and Fraser described that week of fellowship and ministry as the happiest week of his life. When the liberty and joy which characterised the meetings, the warmth of fellowship and the testimonies of God's gracious dealings were reported to the Shanghai leadership, their fears were removed.

Meanwhile reports were being received from many parts of China of a similar moving of the Spirit, of a spiritual hunger and thirst after righteousness and of that thirst being satisfied. One fellow missionary from the spiritually barren north-west who had grown cynical about the professing "Christians" there could hardly believe what he found when he arrived in Shanxi to take up the post of vice-principal at the Hoste School. Never before had he met such vibrant Chinese Christianity, and he had certainly never known so godly a spiritual leader as David Yang, the pastoral superintendent of thirteen counties and a colleague of Elizabeth Fischbacher in his own native city of Quwo.

A few years later, and the long war against Japan would test the strength of the Church to its limits. It was only a God-sent revival that enabled the Church to surmount the severe trials of the Japanese occupation, and only a Church which had known an outpouring of God's Spirit and proved His faithfulness under trial could have faced the greater tribulation under an oppressive Communist government. Revival is seldom primarily for personal enjoyment, and history teaches that the purging fire of renewal is normally a preparation for meeting a fiery trial of suffering. This has certainly been so in the history of the Chinese Church. God visited that Church with revival in each of the first four decades of the century, and each time that visitation proved to be a preparation for future trial or persecution. Does that say something to the churches in the West today?

4 Faith Finds a Way (1934–36)

> "Thy Kingdom come, Thy will be done, on earth
> as it is in heaven."
>
> *Matthew 6:10*

David Yang had a very different background from that of
Wang Mingdao or Watchman Nee, his father being a simple
farmer living in southern Shanxi. In 1900, "the year of the
rat", the Boxers had killed the missionaries who for eleven
years had been building up the church in Farmer Yang's
prefecture. They had also looted and set fire to the homes
of Christians in the city and in the villages, and since Farmer
Yang had been one of the first converts in the district his
was among the families threatened. But amid all the terror
and sorrow of that fateful year the birth of a son had brought
comfort and joy to the parents. (How strange that in that
same terrible year both Wang Mingdao and David Yang
were born, both to become vessels unto honour in God's
house!)

Shaotang (his given name) enjoyed a happy, carefree
childhood after the 1900 terror had passed, as season followed season entering into all the traditional activities of the
small village community. During the long, cold winters,
when he would wear thick cotton-padded garments and a
fur hat, little work could be done in the fields; but with the
coming of spring all the farmers became busy again, sowing,
cultivating and reaping two crops a year: wheat in the
summer and millet, maize or sorghum in the autumn. As
soon as possible the lad from the "Yang-family-village"

began to attend the church school in the city and there learnt to love the Bible. When he was twelve years of age his parents proudly sent him north to attend the Hoste Middle School in Hongdong, where so many future Christian leaders received their education and character training. An exciting new chapter in Shaotang's life, at a school where high academic standards were maintained and a varied programme of sport and religious activities was provided, thus began.

The Hongdong Bible Institute catered largely for the less well-educated, and it trained only evangelists, whereas Shaotang felt called to the ordained ministry. The foremost evangelical theological college in north China was the Presbyterian seminary at Tengxian in Shandong Province, so in 1923, with the help of his parents and the support of his church Shaotang began his theological studies there. But despite all his religious influences up to then it was not until he attended a summer conference in the lovely mountain resort of Guling, high above the Yangzi River, that he entered into full assurance of salvation and adopted for himself the name of David.

David graduated from the seminary in 1925, and then, refusing tempting offers of well-paid employment in the Presbyterian mission, decided to return to his native province to serve the Lord there. His own church at once invited him to become their pastor. He was responsible not only for his own local church in Quwo but for the oversight of the churches in thirteen counties, all of which regularly invited him to speak at their annual and other conferences.

When in 1926, owing to the first Communist uprising, all missionaries were recalled to the coast, the Christians of Shanxi again faced a flood of anti-Christian propaganda which was hard for them to endure. And David Yang, with other leaders, had to think deeply about the future of the Church. In 1928, as the crisis subsided, the missionaries returned, bringing with them the proposals for the churches to become fully autonomous. Some valued Chinese workers, finding the new situation quite unacceptable, decided to leave the province to seek well-paid employment elsewhere. David Yang was naturally confronted with the same dilemma: to go or to stay? In 1931, financial necessity and a need in the Hoste School, of which he was already a governor, took him to Hongdong to be the acting principal, a post which of course carried a salary. In the vacation, however, he continued to speak at church conferences, and that year he took me with him, even allowing me to give my first faltering messages in Chinese. As I travelled and lived with this man I realised I was observing a true man of God, a skilful exponent of Scripture capable of adapting his teaching to suit the agricultural life-style of his hearers, and a wise and much-loved leader.

Following the two visits of the Bethel Band in 1931 and 1933, the second time with Dr John Sung as the leading figure, the churches were never the same again and were beginning to appreciate the wisdom of the Mission's indigenous policy. They were learning to depend more wholly on the Lord rather than on the foreign missionary organisation but they still faced great problems. They were desperately short of well-trained leaders, and under the new conditions even the graduates of the Hongdong Bible Institute could hardly be expected to serve the churches and support their families on the pittance available. Many were therefore asking if there were not some better way ahead.

Returning from Hongdong to his home church, David Yang spent much time in prayer with his missionary colleagues, and God began to reveal to him His plan for the southern region. On one of David's journeys rain turned the motor road into an impassable quagmire and he had to spend several days at an inn waiting for the weather to clear and the road to dry. It was in that crude hostelry that a clear vision of something quite new came to him: that of a team of fellow workers living a communal life of faith, half the year being devoted to prayer, Bible study and investigating the nature of the Christian ministry and the other half spent going out in small teams to the churches and putting into practice the truths learnt while studying together. Young missionaries would also be welcomed as members of the team on a basis of complete equality with their Chinese co-workers. As during a prolonged period of prayer the final pattern of things became clear, David confidently refused a pressing invitation to return to join the staff of his Alma Mater at Tengxian, and the Ling Gong Tuan (Spiritual Work Team) was born. Being an admirer of Watchman Nee's work, David paid a prolonged visit to Shanghai to observe Nee's programme for training his workers.

During the summer of 1934 a cluster of simple buildings constructed of adobe began to rise on land donated for the purpose. The central building was to serve the dual purpose of a lecture room and a refectory, while around it were thirty-four individual rooms for the team members. The entire project was completed in exactly three months, and in September twenty men and women forming the first team began their studies. Revival was in the air, and many, including David Yang himself, were seeking for a special anointing of the Holy Spirit. God was pouring out His blessing everywhere and, at the same time, teaching deep lessons of faith such as Hudson Taylor had once learnt in a similar school of hard experience. God was meeting all the financial needs of the Ling Gong Tuan, which soon developed into a centre of rich spiritual life and activity. Faith had found a way, and the problem of providing Spirit-filled workers for the revived churches had found a solution. Missionaries rejoiced in the way that God was taking things out of their hands, and during that spring of 1935 the future on the spiritual scene looked very bright.

It was enterprises such as this that were preparing the leadership in the churches for the testing times ahead. Early in the war with Japan, missionaries were forced to leave Shanxi never to return. Clearly, as can now be seen so well, a sovereign God was raising up His servants and soldiers to fight the good fight of faith in the fierce spiritual battles yet to come; and in the evil day so soon to break they would stand their ground.

Sadly, in the spring of 1935, the comparative peace which Shanxi had long enjoyed under General Yen Hsi-shan, governor of what had been called the "model province", was rudely shattered. Rumours which circulated quickly that the Communist armies had crossed the Yellow River into that region proved only too true. Nationalist armies sent to oppose them proved helpless against the skilful guerilla tactics of the Communists, who moved rapidly from county to county looting the homes of the wealthy landowners and spreading terror as they went. City after city was threatened, and although the Spiritual Work Team was not molested a passing Communist detachment daubed revolutionary slogans on the outside walls of its premises.

Three of us bachelors were stationed in the nearby city of Xinjiang where, as the Communists approached, the massive city gates were firmly closed as a precaution against an attack or a siege. Untrained militiamen manned the walls, where small museum-piece cannon were placed in the battlements, more to reassure the residents than to terrify the enemy, while captured spies were brought into the city daily to be summarily executed. From the walls we could see the Communist detachments moving freely from hamlet to hamlet; but although no attempt was made to attack the city itself, fear reigned. The press of China, followed by that of the world, reported the capture both of Xinjiang and of the resident missionaries, to the deep concern of the Mission authorities and of our relatives. Hongdong was less fortunate, and a comic medieval-style siege, with the Communists using scaling ladders to assault the walls (unsuccessfully, as it turned out) and the defenders setting up dummies as decoys to draw the enemy fire, was staged. Inside the city were a dozen missionaries who anxiously awaited the outcome of the battle. They too were reported as being "in Communist hands", for reporters always failed to distinguish between the county boundaries and the county city itself: the county might be and often was in Communist hands, but this was rarely the case with the city of the same name. Failing to capture the cities, the Communist forces moved rapidly north, content with looting the wealth of the countryside as they went. Eventually life returned to normal, but in Tokyo the alarm signals were ringing, since with the Communists over the Yellow River the Japanese military presence in Peking was being threatened. War therefore became inevitable, and the Church in Shanxi would never again enjoy the peace and liberty it had known hitherto; everywhere, indeed, the death-knell of freedom was sounding. What lessons was God seeking to teach both Chinese and missionaries through experiences such as these?

In the summer of 1935 the annual district convention of the southern Shanxi churches was held in a beautifully situated mountain temple. David Yang, in the opening meeting, announced his theme as Revelation 1:9: "I, John, your brother, who share with you in Jesus the tribulation and the kingdom and the patient endurance", and the burden of his preaching in the days that followed was the need for brokenness if the experience of the Spirit's fullness was to be maintained. St. Paul wrote of his own experiences in 2 Corinthians 2:14: "Thanks be to God who always leadeth me about as a prisoner in the train of His triumph!" Paul's proud self had been conquered and broken. His words might be paraphrased: "I was once proud, self-willed, self-opinionated, self-pitying, self-exalting, but Christ over-mastered me. He broke me down and subdued my stubborn spirit." David Yang emphasised that the believer must know the experience of the Cross in daily life and needs to be totally abandoned to God's disciplinary processes – an attitude which would certainly involve a common sharing in tribulation, in the Kingdom and in patient endurance. Little did the speaker realise how prophetic his words would prove to be and how, like John the Divine, he himself at the end of his life would experience in a poignant way the fellowship of Christ's sufferings on account of his loyalty to his Lord in the face of Communist persecution. This message also penetrated deeply into my heart at a time of acute personal crisis. I had just seen my fiancée invalided home with little chance of returning to China – the answer to my prayer for brokenness?

A year later, while on leave in England, I stayed with my old school friends the Church family, who lived outside Cambridge. Dr Joe Church, one of the leading figures in the East Africa revival, was then at home, and we were able to compare the course of the revivals in Africa and those in China. Naturally they had many features in common: the conviction of sin and the painful process of repentance, the need for a broken and a contrite spirit at all times, the joys of cleansing and forgiveness, the new release and freedom in personal relationships, the burning desire for the Spirit's fullness and the ever-present dangers of satanic counterfeits and emotional extremes. It was a great privilege, during that first leave spent in the USA, Canada and then Britain, to have been a witness of God's mighty acts in China just before the storm broke and to report how He was preparing as the leaders of His Church there men like David Yang: men who would endure as seeing Him who is invisible and who through faith would face torture and suffer mockery, beating, even chains and imprisonment; men "of whom the world is not worthy".

5   The Maelstrom of War (1937–45)

> "We thank Thee, Lord God almighty, that Thou hast taken Thy great power and begun to reign. The nations raged, but Thy wrath came."
>
> *Revelation 11:17*

World War II originated in Peking, China. Japan under the generals and Germany under Hitler had everything in common: racial pride, imperialist ambitions and a powerful military machine. First Japan invaded China; then Germany invaded Poland. The next step was Pearl Harbour, when Japan challenged the USA and became an ally of Germany, while Germany challenged the might of Russia. Finally, as Japan faced imminent defeat by the Western Allies, Russia, like a hungry vulture, cynically declared war on a prostrate Japan in order to share in the spoils of war in the Far East.

That war, for all missionaries, was a hazardous, sometimes exciting but often costly experience. What it did was afford the opportunity to identify with the Chinese people in their suffering and to serve them in a wide variety of ways. For Chinese Christians the war was a time of testing, because missionaries in east China who avoided internment by making their way to west China left the churches on their own. Had revival prepared them sufficiently for such a situation? The answer was undoubtedly "Yes", for Christians displayed great courage and endurance under the Japanese occupation, and when the war ended missionaries found that in their suffering the churches had grown to greater maturity. The experiences described in this chapter can be regarded as a small sample of what both missionaries and Chinese Christians endured through eight years of war.

During our first leave my wife, wonderfully restored to full health, and I were married in Philadelphia, USA. She was a granddaughter of C. H. Judd, one of Hudson Taylor's closest colleagues, and we had first met at our Shanxi summer resort. During that leave events in China began to unfold in an ominous way. Finally, in 1937, on the "double seventh" (July 7th), the first shots of a war which would ultimately engulf the world were fired at the Marco Polo Bridge outside Peking. Shortly after the birth of our first child we returned to China. Passing through Japan, we travelled on a hospital train, for the ashes of the dead, in little white boxes, were already coming home, along with the wounded, from the battlefields of China. As we sailed up the Huangpu River to Shanghai, the devastation of war was only too apparent on both banks, where mere ruins remained of once prosperous villages.

Japan's rulers had always entertained grandiose plans for imperial conquest. Its armies had occupied and annexed Formosa in 1895 and Korea in 1910, the latter being forced to become a servile subject nation. The 1919 Treaty of Versailles had awarded the Japanese, in recognition of their help in defeating Germany, the former German possessions in China, Qingdao and the Shandong Peninsula. Although the Chinese had protested angrily, their protests had been ignored. In 1931, defying world opinion, Japanese armies marched into Manchuria and began to threaten Peking. The Chinese people were helpless: all they could do was conduct violent anti-Japanese agitation and a boycott of Japanese goods. The Japanese replied by attacking Shanghai, China's nerve-centre. At Christmas 1936 Generalissimo Chiang Kai-shek flew to Xian to direct the campaign against the Communist armies but was promptly kidnapped by a pro-Communist general and held prisoner until a promise was extracted from him to end mere passive resistance and actively to oppose Japanese aggression and encroachment. War then ensued, and Japan embarked on her master plan to establish a "Greater East Asia Co-Prosperity Sphere" according to which she would be the industrial base providing all Asia needed in the way of manufactured goods while the rest of that continent would become a vast rice-bowl providing for the food needs of half the world.

Arriving back in Shanghai, we found a beautiful and spacious new headquarters of the China Inland Mission. The original Woosung Road premises had been reduced to rubble by Japanese shell fire only weeks after the move to this new address had been made – just in time! Soon we were on our way to the war zone in north China. In Hebei, four armies were on the march: the Japanese regular army, which was already holding all the main cities and the lines of communication; a Chinese puppet army supporting that army; the Nationalist army seeking to fight set-piece battles with Japanese armies and the Communist guerilla units, which were constantly harrying the enemy everywhere and successfully attacking and disrupting the Japanese lines of communication.

Those who suffered most were the helpless villagers who lived only for their land and their animals, eking out a precarious living. Traditionally soldiers were wicked people, as the Chinese proverb says: "You don't use good iron to make nails and you don't use good men to make soldiers!" It mattered little what army it was, it came to hurt and destroy; so the villagers were always on the alert and ready to flee at the approach of any military, leaving their few possessions behind. Christians, however, often prepared cloth bags to hold their precious Bibles, and these at least they took with them. In a land where shelves loaded with reference books were an unknown luxury for ministers, Christians were people of one book only – the Bible. Since the majority even of Christians were illiterate, the Bible was their only textbook, teaching them the truths about creation and the world around them. In the absence of public libraries the Bible was also their sole recreational reading, providing fascinating stories from ancient history, poetry and philosophy. But, primarily, the Bible was their only book of devotion, revealing Christ in His fullness as the divine answer to man's personal and social needs, promising him forgiveness of sin, fellowship with God and the assurance of eternal life. In the turmoil of war, Christians learned to treasure this book more than ever before; it was their most precious possession. Many passages were set to music and sung and so became the memory hymnbooks of the future, when bibles and hymnals would be confiscated and destroyed. Passages were also memorised chapter by chapter so that during long years spent in prison or labour camps without a Bible church leaders would sustain their spiritual lives through the Word of God hidden within their hearts.

Hwailu was the administrative centre for the China Inland Mission field in the province of Hebei, where churches existed in seven or eight of the counties and missionaries were resident in three or four of the prefectural cities. It was my responsibility to visit both churches and missionaries to bring encouragement, fellowship and advice where needed. The kind of emergency which arose was when the Christians in one town reported that the Japanese unit there had turned the chapel into a brothel and installed Korean prostitutes. I immediately hurried on my bicycle to lodge a strong protest with the local commander, demanding that the chapel be cleared of the women immediately and arguing that the property was actually owned by a British organisation. The officer saw the point, and the chapel was handed back to the Christians.

Wherever one travelled, danger lurked on every hand. Bursts of rifle or machine-gun fire constantly broke the silence, and on approaching any city by dusk there was the frequent glint of steel and the uncertainty of one's reception. Meanwhile, a faithful band of Chinese men and women were bravely carrying on their work of evangelism and pastoral visitation, putting into practice in hard times the lessons of courage and persistence learned in earlier days.

Our short spell of service in Hebei completed, we were asked to move to east Shanxi to assume similar responsibilities. In Luan, the main city of the region, the China Inland

Mission hospital had a staff of three doctors – a man and two women – and three nurses. Of the five main cities four had resident missionaries. In the same area was the station where Gladys Aylward ("the small woman" of the book of that title and heroine of the film *The Inn of the Sixth Happiness*) and her senior missionary, David Davies, lived. A Japanese column had previously fought its way into the region but, after suffering heavy casualties, had been forced to withdraw. Now the region was considered likely to enjoy freedom from any further Japanese offensive for at least a year, so we prepared to make the six-day journey through Nationalist or guerrilla-controlled territory to Luan. The route was precisely the one followed in reverse by Archibald Glover and his party in 1900 when escaping from the Boxers, a journey described so vividly in *A Thousand Miles of Miracle*.[1]

Medicines and petroleum for the hospital had to be purchased. Twenty mules with their muleteers had to be hired to carry our own boxes and the hospital supplies. Two mules carried the litter shaded by straw matting in which travelled my wife Kathryn, six months pregnant, and our one-year-old daughter. A Union Jack covered the litter, and another waved from the saddle of the leading mule: a precaution against possible Japanese strafing from the air and a reassurance to any Chinese units we might meet en route. We knew that Japanese planes frequently bombed the cities through which we were to pass. A Chinese evangelist from Luan was our escort, even taking his turn in carrying the family canary in its cage!

Finally, on a bright spring morning in 1939 we said goodbye to our friends and set off to the crack of whips and the sound of many hoofs clattering on the cobbled streets. At the last Japanese outpost the officer inspected our papers and allowed us to proceed. Now the atmosphere in no man's land, with few people in evidence, became eerie, and within a short while we passed a man lying dead by the roadside – a gruesome sight from which I tried to divert my wife's attention. But fruit trees in blossom and fields green with the early growth of spring wheat were a delight. In the late afternoon we reached the first walled city on our route and were thankful for the Union Jacks, which assured the defending Chinese troops on the walls that we were friendly. The local missionaries had long since left, but we were able to enjoy the comparative comfort of their home for the night.

Every subsequent night was spent in an inn on a hard brick *kang* with the inevitable bugs and fleas to contend with. Villagers swarmed around to stare at us, poke holes in the paper windows and watch our every action – and in their eyes our fair-haired child was strange-looking indeed. Each night the mules had to be unloaded and fed and each morning reloaded ready for an early start, so we too had to rise before dawn to eat a hurried breakfast. I sometimes rode my own mule and sometimes walked, while our small daughter, when weary of sitting in the enclosed litter, either rode or walked with me for a change. The rough roads had been deeply trenched at intervals so as to hinder any further intrusion by Japanese wheeled vehicles and this meant frequent switchback effects for the litter and its occupants! Once at the end of a long day, finding the only inn to be full, we had to go on to the next village. In the darkness a sudden storm blew up frightening the mules, which attempted to bolt so that the shafts of the litter became dislodged. It was a moment of anxiety, but the muleteers quickly brought the animals under control and no one suffered harm.

On the third day we knew we were entering guerilla territory when we reached a village where small boys armed with long poles and with a severe look of authority challenged us. Once our identity was known the guerillas gave us a warm welcome, and in one village we discovered Christians among them. On the sixth and last day we reached the second mission station where, after living on Chinese food for a week, we enjoyed a "foreign" noon meal, for here we found fellow missionaries in residence. This couple were to be of great service to us in the coming Japanese occupation, receiving mail from the secret Chinese Post Office in the hills and forwarding it to us by regular messengers.

Urged by the muleteers not to delay, we hurried on. The final ten miles of our journey were covered in the dark, so we were delighted to be met and escorted to our destination by Gordon Anderson, the doctor in charge at Luan. Six days of rough and hazardous travel were at an end.

Our new home was the identical building in which C. T. Studd and Stanley Smith of the Cambridge Seven had once lived. Because the house was supposed to be haunted, the "foreign devils" had been allowed to take possession. The Glovers had lived there up to 1900 to be followed by a succession of missionaries of whom we were to be the last. We were soon introduced to Gordon Anderson's wife Marjorie, and to "wee" Marjorie who would be a companion for our daughter.

We noticed huge Union Jacks painted on all the roofs of the hospital to warn Japanese planes not to bomb foreign neutrals. (The outbreak of war in the Pacific was still in the future.) At that time Communist units commanded by the legendary Marshal Zhu De controlled the countryside, and his wife was once brought into the hospital for treatment. The marshal also asked advice from the doctor about homosexuality among his men. In gratitude for the services of the hospital he presented the doctors with an antique vase.

We lost no time in getting into the work of preaching and teaching the church people and visiting the Christians in the villages. Pastor Chang Mengen was an old friend from the west of the province and is now, in 1984, still serving the Lord as one of the team in the Three-Self church in Lanzhou, Gansu. My first round of visits to the missionaries in the "parish" was made by bicycle, and I found all was fairly peaceful and everyone was getting on with the work normally – but then the unexpected happened.

In May we and the Andersons, including the three small girls, celebrated my wife's birthday with a happy picnic in a lovely country spot amid the scent of wild roses. The photo I took of that group proved to be the last to be taken of Gordon, for soon afterwards he contracted typhoid fever and, tragically, did not recover. To Chinese and missionaries

alike Gordon's death was a shock and a serious loss at such
a time. It fell to me to conduct the funeral service and to make
arrangements for the escort of the coffin to the Christian
cemetery in a neighbouring city. Later Marjorie and her
two children left for Peking and Scotland, leaving us acutely
aware that missionary work has always been a costly enter-
prise. Hundreds of doctors and other missionaries have
sacrificed their lives in order that the Good News might be
shared with the Chinese people.

Then the bombing began! None of the cities had any
anti-aircraft protection, and when the temple bell sounded
the warning of the approach of enemy planes we made at
once for the hospital cellar, our only shelter. After one raid
the pastor and I visited a village where a Christian home
had been wrecked to offer our comfort and to give such
practical aid as we could. As air raids increased in frequency
it became evident that the Japanese were planning, much
sooner than we had been led to expect, a second offensive
into our region. Realising this, the local commander ordered
the city to be totally evacuated, leaving behind nothing
whatever for the enemy – no food, no livestock, just the
empty shell of the city. He tried to persuade us to leave
with him, but we pleaded our neutrality. In order to make
provision for a possible siege of indefinite duration I went
into the country to procure several milch cows and supplies
of grain. David Davies came over to discuss plans. Together
we visited the Roman Catholic mission and its friendly
Dutch bishop who, sadly, was to be killed by the Communists a few years later. David and I looked rather enviously
at the fruit and vegetable gardens and the vineyards which
flourished in that part of the city where there was sweet
water in the wells; in our section the well water was brackish,
so that we had to buy drinking-water from water carts and
could grow very little.

On July 6th, while we were enjoying breakfast in the
garden, the temple bell again sounded the urgent alarm and
we hurried down to the cellar. As the bombers flew roof
high over the city, bombing their targets at will, my wife's

labour pains began. No sooner had the all-clear sounded than she went into hospital and quickly gave birth to a baby girl. An hour later, the planes returned. As the mother could not be moved, the infant was placed under the bed while she lay watching the planes flying low on their deadly mission. Emerging from our shelter we found shrapnel scattered everywhere; but little damage had been done and, mercifully, mother and babe were safe.

The nurse wondered, under the circumstances, what suitable diet she could provide for the nursing mother. The shops were all empty and shuttered. Only the barking of hungry dogs disturbed the uncanny silence of a dead city. The hospital and church buildings were surrounded by a wall, outside which were cultivated fields. So imagine the nurse's astonishment when one morning she heard the squawking of a chicken in the courtyard. It had flown over the wall and was most probably the only one left in a deserted city, for no Chinese family would leave behind a precious hen! This was God's timely provision for a very special need.

A day or two later came the moment of the expected attack. Suddenly the sound of gunfire broke the silence, and after the city gates had been easily forced, cavalry charged up and down every street firing rifles and sub-machine-guns. They were followed by a column of infantry, one of whose officers paid us a courtesy visit when we assured him of our neutrality. One of the missionaries was a German lady who hung her swastika flag side by side with our Union Jack outside the compound gate, a sight which the Japanese found highly amusing, even though Britain and Germany were not yet at war. Daily and with growing anxiety we listened to the world news on our hidden radio.

The Japanese army quickly settled down, even though at first, with all ground communications cut, they had to be supplied by air. It was only the kindness of the Roman Catholic bishop that kept us supplied with vegetables and fruit. Every day he used to send a small boy with a basket of good things which we shared among the several households, rejoicing that God still, as in Elijah's day, had His ravens to obey His commands.

Slowly the city came to life again: Korean merchants arrived to open watch and camera shops for the benefit of the Japanese troops, and Korean women were brought in as prostitutes. One by one the Chinese merchants plucked up courage to return, and gradually things became fairly normal. I endeavoured to maintain good relations with the military police, and successive Japanese commanding officers paid us courtesy visits. A Christian medical officer became a good friend. Back at home in Japan his wife had given birth to a child at the same time as mine, and so he came in as often as possible to see our child's development, thinking of his own infant whom he had never seen.

The occupation did not go unchallenged by the Chinese, and night after night we heard bursts of machine-gun fire directed at the guards at the gates. When we smelt burning flesh we knew that there had been a cremation of the dead following a fierce engagement. One evening a Chinese knocked at the compound gate and was admitted. He claimed to be a spy for the Chinese armies and to be afraid of sleeping in the city; he was sure that we, as friends of China, would give him safe lodging for the night. As the pastor and I talked with him we grew suspicious, and finally we threatened to report him to the Japanese police if he did not leave. It was just as well that we did, for he proved to be an *agent provocateur* sent to trap us.

Then one day a young Japanese private who we discovered had been associated with the Japan Evangelistic Band mission hall in Kobe rushed in hot from the battlefield to warn us that street fighting in a neighbouring city where three lady missionaries were living was placing them in great danger. He urged us to bring them out at once. So, after borrowing two mules (without pack saddles) from the military hospital, the pastor and I took on the role of muleteers. To the sound of constant automatic fire we made the day-long journey to the war-torn city, whose ancient walls had been broken down by the Chinese to render it less defensible.

The Japanese major in command, a genial Roman Catholic and an artist, received me courteously and at once authorised the departure of the ladies. However, we declined his invitation to travel with the daily convoy which we knew came under regular fire from Chinese guerillas. Early the next morning as the major sat sketching on the ruins of the city walls he found the sight of our party setting out quite hilarious. It consisted of two badly laden mules and their drivers, one foreign lady with a Chinese carrying-pole and its balanced loads, another pushing a bicycle loaded with her indispensable stove-pipes, a blind gatekeeper with his carrying-pole and all his worldly goods and his small son herding a flock of goats! Nervously, with dusk falling, we approached the Luan city gates. The others were allowed home, but I spent the night in the gatehouse eating roast corn cobs with the Japanese guards.

The subsequent arrest of my colleague, the pastor, and the hospital evangelist involved me in constant protests for two weeks before securing their release. Meanwhile the Japanese had succeeded in extending the railway from the provincial capital right to Luan. As the children had never seen a railway engine, I asked my friend in the military police for a permit to take the family outside the city to see the trains. Foolishly, I took my camera with me and was observed photographing the girls walking along the rails. But was I not photographing "military installations"? So I was politely arrested, while the family were sent home wondering when they might see me again. Shortly a captain arrived to give me a fierce dressing-down in the presence of the junior officer who had arrested me. But, in the providence of God, when the latter had left the signal box where I was being held, the captain told me that he too was a Christian and the son of a pastor. All would be well, he said, but I must be more careful in the future. Within three hours, to everyone's relief, I was back home, but without the film in my camera. David Davies was less fortunate. After a Chinese evangelist had escorted Gladys Aylward and her orphans safely across the Yellow River into Shaanxi Province, her reports of Japanese atrocities, published in the foreign press, reached the Japanese themselves; as a result, David was first tortured and then taken in chains to an internment camp where he remained for the next five years.

World news was worsening, and war in the Pacific seemed more and more certain. Orders from Shanghai to withdraw from Luan reached us. Everyone was notified, and an orderly departure was arranged. I preached my last sermon on St. Paul's farewell message to the Ephesian elders – so very appropriate. Early on a bitterly cold winter morning we said goodbye to our Chinese friends. The children threw their arms around the neck of their amah, a loved and lovely Christian woman. At the railway station we found the staff warming themselves at an open fire on the platform and were glad to join them. To our great surprise the head of the military police, whom I had sometimes helped in various ways, arrived with a small detachment of men to see us off in polite Japanese style! On the first stage of our journey we travelled in an unheated goods wagon and were more than thankful for the warm fur coats for the children which had arrived, through the secret Post Office, all the way from Canada, just a few days before we were to leave – another miracle of God's timing.

We were genuinely sad to leave Luan and our Christian friends there and could only imagine what difficulties and dangers lay ahead of them. But among the several hundred believers God had His faithful servants both in the city and in the villages, and they were well grounded in the Word of God. Confirmation that God reigns came in 1982, when we received direct from Luan news to the effect that, after the harsh Japanese occupation followed by decades of atheist indoctrination, the number of Christians in the region had increased to over a thousand and that in spite of much suffering the former hospital staff were still going on with the Lord and God was blessing His people. The local government doctor was one of the students converted in Peking in my medical school Bible class and was now ministering to the various Christian groups. The roots of this living church reached right back to the pioneer work of Studd and Stanley Smith; many others in the following years had nurtured the growing plant, and their labours had not been in vain.

On reaching Peking we renewed acquaintance with our friends Wang Mingdao and David Yang. The Japanese authorities were demanding the unification of all Protestant churches and in so doing were anticipating future Communist policies. But Wang Mingdao had adamantly refused to allow his congregation to join this amalgamation, and when the Japanese threatened his life he told them he had already bought his coffin just in case! Years later Mr Wang was to show the same resolution when facing the Communist authorities and their agents; but meanwhile, within the limitations of enemy occupation and a nation at war, he was carrying on his powerful ministry of preaching, teaching and writing. David Yang, too, following the termination of the work of the Spiritual Work Team, had left Shanxi and was continuing a Bible teaching ministry on a smaller scale.

For everyone, Chinese and foreigners alike, the seven years of war were dark and difficult and the future was always shrouded in total uncertainty. But spiritual giants like Wang Mingdao and David Yang never doubted God's love, wisdom or power. They believed that God reigns and that "mightier than the thunders of many waters, mightier than the waves of the sea, the Lord on high is mighty." Believing that God was working out His own purposes for China and for the world, Mr Wang loved to sing, both then and later during his long years of imprisonment by the Communists:

> All the way my Saviour leads me
> What have I to ask beside?
> Can I doubt His tender mercy
> Who through life has been my Guide?
> Heavenly peace, divinest comfort,
> Here by faith in Him to dwell!
> For I know whate'er befall me
> Jesus doeth all things well.

6 China's Lifeline (1940)

"As I live, says the Lord, every knee shall bow to
Me, and every tongue shall give praise to God."

Romans 14:11

In the face of the brutal invasion by Japanese armies the
Chinese, with minimum air cover, fought bravely against
vastly superior forces and actually won several famous victories. But, inexorably, the Japanese war machine drove the
Nationalist armies further and further west, while in eastern
China the Communist guerillas continued to harry the forces
of occupation. By 1939 the Japanese were in control of all
the major cities in the east, including Nanjing, the Chinese
capital. The Nationalists had established an emergency
capital in Chongqing in west China.

This Japanese conquest set in motion one of the greatest
migrations in history, when sixty million people fled from
occupied territory to "free China" in the west. People from
all walks of life left their homes and businesses to continue
to live in freedom in the country's more backward provinces.
The sophisticated residents of Peking, Shanghai or Canton
found life there so primitive that they marvelled how foreign
missionaries could have endured such living conditions: no
electricity, no sewage system, no running water and no
entertainment other than the traditional Chinese theatre.
The local people, for their part, resented the influx of the
"down-river" people with their incomprehensible dialects
who began to take away their business and their trade.

China's future clearly depended on her youth. Realising

this, the government ordered all educational institutions that could possibly do so to join the trek to the west. So universities packed up their libraries, laboratories and scientific equipment and transported them by river boat or along totally inadequate roads to Sichuan, Yunnan, Guizhou, Shaanxi and Gansu Provinces, where they either commandeered temples or put up army-style huts as provisional university and college accommodation, a stark contrast to the beautiful campuses they had left behind.

It is easy to see the sovereign wisdom and purpose of God in this great movement of people. Up to the outbreak of war there had been virtually no evangelical student work in China: work among students had been the monopoly of the theologically liberal and politically left-wing YMCA. Now, for the first time, students desiring to improve their English or looking for some of the cultural interests they had left behind met with missionaries of an evangelical persuasion who eagerly seized the new opportunities and arranged Bible classes for them. Chinese evangelists found the young people to be very receptive audiences and eventually a Chinese Inter-Varsity Fellowship was formed under the leadership of Calvin Chao who, in 1945, called the first national conference held in Chongqing. Thus among students the seeds were sown of a post-war revival which was to have very far-reaching consequences for the Chinese Church. Yes, the Lord, who makes all things work together for good, reigns.

Anticipating the total blockade of the Chinese coastal ports, the Chinese government embarked on the extremely difficult engineering project of constructing a motor highway from Burma over high mountain ranges to Kunming, the capital of Yunnan Province, which was also the base for the airlift of military supplies from India. The Burma road had been built with heavy loss of life among the engineers and workmen who had blasted their way forward with tremendous urgency. This highway became China's only lifeline, and as soon as it was completed volunteers had patriotically come from all over the world to drive trucks laden with all kinds of essential supplies from Rangoon, through the Shan

States, on into China and so to Kunming. From there the road continued through Guizhou Province into Sichuan Province and finally to Chongqing, the wartime capital. Under very favourable conditions the journey from Rangoon to Chongqing by petrol-driven vehicle would have taken at least ten days, but under unfavourable conditions and by a crawling charcoal-burning truck it could take a month or more. One such truck was christened "Genesis" by its Friends' Ambulance Unit drivers in Rangoon, only to be renamed "Revelation" on finally reaching its destination!

For many missionaries the Burma road became the only route into China, and all had their own stories to tell of hair-raising journeys. So when in 1940 Bishop Frank Houghton, the new general director of the CIM, greeted us on arrival in Shanghai from the north after leaving Luan and Shanxi and appointed us to the city of Anshun in Guizhou, we too faced the prospect of journeys on this notorious highway. The bishop described the situation in Anshun as constituting perhaps the greatest challenge in west China. The mission hospital there was doing good work, he told us, but the church had totally disintegrated and an entirely new beginning would have to be made. There were two refugee colleges there and other refugee colleges in nearby towns, so the opportunities promised to be great.

In planning our journeys from Shanghai we thought it wise for my wife and the two girls to travel by air from Hong Kong to Chongqing and then south by bus to Anshun while I, with the heavy baggage, would go by sea to Rangoon and from there up the Burma road to join them. As I arrived in Rangoon the city was taking feverish anti-airraid precautions. Nevertheless the water festival of Thingtan, the Burmese New Year, was being celebrated with the usual gay abandon: everybody dousing water over everybody else on the streets and on the trams and buses. Young men, stripped to the waist, bore inscriptions on their backs and chests, one such reading "If the country does not care, why should I?" All too soon Burma itself would be engulfed in war. What then? Would they care?

A search for transport into China was rewarded when a
French adventurer and his Chinese companion agreed to
take me and my goods as far as Kunming. The original
convoy, bound for Chongqing, consisted of two new trucks
assembled in Rangoon and loaded with valuable cargoes, a
Pontiac saloon and a Studebaker saloon in which I was to
travel with M. Mazurie and his companion, to be sold at
journey's end at a fantastic profit. Add to these vehicles a
comfortable caravan, complete with ice box, which was to
provide luxury sleeping accommodation for the three of us
all the way. After endless delays due to red tape, we said
goodbye to Rangoon (described by Adoniram Judson,
Burma's first pioneer missionary, as that "sad, silly city")
and set off cheerfully and hopefully on the long trek.

But the first of many misadventures was not long in
overtaking us when, in a tropical downpour, we watched
with horror the caravan, which was being towed by one of
the trucks, break away from its too-weak coupling and career
down a steep bank into a rice paddy. That was already the
end of our planned luxury travel; thereafter accommodation
was perforce to be mostly in Chinese inns and hotels, good
and bad. As we left the "road to Mandalay" and turned
east through the Shan States, the road ran through dense,
rotting jungle where big game lurked amid the teak, redwood
and tree ferns; but as we climbed steeply up to 3,000 feet in
nineteen miles, the air became cool and fresh and the scenery
magnificent. Colourfully clad Shan women carried loaded
baskets on their heads, while the men were tattooed heavily
all over their bodies. At Loilem roses bloomed in the gardens,
the sparkle of fireflies lit up the evening gloom and bells
hanging from the Buddhist temple eaves tinkled in the
breeze.

At last our convoy rolled into Lashio, the booming border
town where the local people were making fortunes out of the
international traffic. Lashio was a link in the chain of airports
linking London and Hong Kong and continuing by "China
Clipper" over the Pacific to the USA. Here misfortune
continued to dog our steps, for one of the trucks was found

to have been incorrectly registered and Mazurie had to go back to Bhamo to deal with the matter. Then "Bulbul" (Fatty), one of the Burmese drivers, while entertaining a girlfriend, was involved in a crash with the Pontiac. Thus we faced an indefinite delay. I found accommodation with the local district officer, an Oxford graduate, in the comfortable government bungalow. On May 1st three senior Indian army officers on a tour of inspection of the frontier defences joined us, bringing their commissariat with them in a separate van. I shared their sumptuous repast and in return introduced them to the mysteries and delights of a Chinese banquet.

The monsoon threatened to break in torrents of rain and our delay foreboded danger ahead on China's unmetalled roads. In Burma the roads had been good, but the 500 miles ahead of us between Lashio and Kunming were among the most hazardous in the world. Writhing like a snake, the road twisted and turned as it climbed gradients so steep that at one point twenty-four and at another seventy-two consecutive hairpin bends had to be hewn out of the mountainside – each bend displaying a skull and crossbones warning! At the highest point in the Wuliang Range the road reached 7,300 feet above sea level. From these dizzy heights it would plunge suddenly down into deep, dark ravines where the mighty Salween and Mekong Rivers were roaring their way from Tibet to the Indian and Pacific Oceans. A first-time traveller on the road could be excused for being horrified at the sight of the burnt-out wrecks of countless trucks littering the verges and the precipitous slopes on either side of the road from start to finish. Drivers had notoriously tried to economise on fuel by switching off the engines on the steep downhill slopes; too often the brakes had seized up and disaster had followed. The loss of life was quite appalling.

Mazurie returned from Bhamo empty-handed so that all that remained of the original convoy was one truck and one saloon car! As we finally left Burma, dark clouds gathered, the heavens burst and trucks skidded dangerously in the liquid mud. We were now in the Chinese province of Yunnan, whose name means "south of the clouds". It was a rain-drenched world with mists filling the deep chasms beneath us. The farther we travelled, the greater was our admiration for the brilliant engineering which had made this wonderful highway possible.

After making the descent to the River Salween, where the bridge had been a frequent target of Japanese planes, we hurried on to reach Baoshan late at night. Sleepy missionaries welcomed us and gave us hospitality. Baoshan was then the centre of Christian work among the Lisu tribe living between the Salween and Mekong Rivers; indeed, the whole mountain region of Burma and south-west China, through which the highway runs, is populated by numerous mountain tribes, but it was the Lisu who had turned to Christ in such large numbers. When the Communists in their conquest of China eventually reached the south-west, many Lisu Christians escaped across the high mountain passes into north Burma where they settled and established thriving churches. They have since been provided with their own translation of the entire Bible, and some of their well-educated young men have become graduates of the theological college in Rangoon.

A theological and a practical problem has always faced missionaries, especially those working among animistic tribes. Though virtually no mass movements to Christianity have occurred among Hindus or Buddhists, tribal animists have quite commonly turned from their spirit worship to Christianity in large numbers. Early missionaries initially made the mistake of supposing that the destruction of demon altars and other paraphernalia was in itself an evidence of "regeneration"; when, in sickness or misfortune, many of their "converts" reverted to spirit worship, these missionaries were disappointed and perplexed. This experience raises such questions as: "At what point does real conversion occur?", "What are the essential evidences of new life in Christ?", "When should Christian baptism take place?" It was not only in the early days that these problems presented themselves, for missionaries today, in north Thailand and elsewhere, are still deeply exercised about the answers. Now, in 1984, it is apparent that many among the hundreds of Hmong tribespeople from Laos in Thai refugee camps who have destroyed their objects of demon worship and been welcomed into the church are unregenerate. And workers among aboriginal tribes are not the only ones to meet with this difficulty: it is, for instance, an equally vexed question in Indonesia, where large numbers of people have been received into the church even though they secretly retain their fetishes and continue their animistic practices. The much publicised "revival" on the Indonesian island of Timor was not so much a revival among believing Christians as the conversion of professing Christians who had been convicted of the sin of secretly worshipping the spirits and who later repented and were born again of the Spirit. Even J. O. Fraser, the great apostle to the Lisu, as a young man in his early twenties had to learn by bitter experience that the destruction of idols was no certain evidence of regeneration.

Dan Smith, a colleague of J. O. Fraser's, after years of experience among the Lisu, came to the conclusion that tribal converts could be divided into three categories (or "dispensations", as he quaintly called them): those who have turned to God from idols and who are God-worshippers but who are not yet regenerate, which describes the vast majority; at this stage many do, for various reasons, revert to animism, since there has been no true repentance and no regenerating work of the Spirit – just a change of ritual without a change of heart. Secondly, there are those who have had a genuine experience of the new birth, who have repented and turned from their sin to find forgiveness and redemption through the Cross of Christ – a comparatively small minority. And finally there are those who are living holy, victorious lives in the fullness of the Holy Spirit – and these, said Dan Smith, are very few indeed. There is no doubt that this analysis of the situation applies all over the world. The restriction of baptism to those in the second category alone provides a sound foundation for a living, growing church. Fortunately for the future of the churches among the Lisu and other tribes, the message of repentance and the need for the new birth had reached them in the 1930s; it would have been a very different story otherwise. As it is, the Lisu and other tribal churches, in spite of the severe persecution they have endured, are today well known to the Communist government as among the largest Christian communities in China.

After Baoshan we made the crossing of the River Mekong before climbing again to stupendous heights until suddenly the fabled city of Dali met our gaze – a lovely, mountain-girt place of alpine splendour on the shores of a lake thirty miles long, the Lake Lucerne of China, with snow covering the summits of the 14,000-feet-high peaks. Dali had been a dream of my youth, as remote as Tibet and many months distant from Shanghai by the old methods of travel. This city had first been visited by a Westerner when John McCarthy of the China Inland Mission passed through on his epic journey across China from east to west, a journey described in advance as "foolish and impossible". He had travelled up the Changjiang (Yangzi) as far as Chongqing in Sichuan before turning south to Dali; from there he had gone on to Bhamo in Burma, a journey of 3,000 miles in seven months, the last half being spent on foot, preaching Christ all the way. This had been in 1877; yet here was I, in a modern automobile, driving up to the gates of the Dali mission station just ten days after leaving Rangoon!

In Dali we learnt that the war in Europe was going badly for Britain, and a young Standard Oil agent at the filling station remarked: "I guess England has taken nearly as much as she should. It's time we sent a million Texas Rangers over. They're tough and a match for any Germans!" We would love to have lingered in Dali but pressed on to Yunnanyi, where Americans were training Chinese air force pilots. Then, when the battery of our car was obviously not charging, we knew our troubles were by no means over. As night fell the headlights failed on a stretch of road where the corners and the hairpin bends seemed to grow more and

more difficult to negotiate. "Je ne vois rien du tout!" shouted
Mazurie at the wheel, cursing the vehicle with a vocabulary
of rich French invective. Yawning depths awaited any false
move, and so it was to my relief when the engine finally
gave up and the car spluttered to a halt. The Chinese
assistant was dispatched to the next town to recall the truck,
while Mazurie and I stayed with the saloon and tried to
snatch a few hours' sleep. We were too weary to bother
about the fact that bandits looking for just such victims as
ourselves infested those parts. Eventually the truck returned
and the battery was charged, and at dawn we were on the
final stage of our journey to Kunming, beautifully situated
beside yet another huge lake forty miles long.

Thanks to the war, Kunming had become a cosmopolitan
city with people of all nationalities thronging its ancient
streets. It enjoyed many modern facilities and great prosperity, though inevitably it had suffered extensive damage
from regular bombing raids. The population had become
used to spending the morning awaiting the warning sirens
and then, as enemy planes approached, making a hasty exodus
to the surrounding countryside, returning to begin the day's
business in the late afternoon. After the long journey from
Rangoon, the China Inland Mission centre provided a quiet
haven of rest. The news awaiting me of the safe arrival of
my family at Anshun was a great relief. I parted from
Mazurie in Kunming and went in search of transport on to
Anshun. This time the only vehicle I could locate was an
old truck much the worse for wear, its engine parts held
together by wire! My three companions had once trained
for the Chinese air force, but such was the state of national
morale that, finding service pay inadequate, they were now,
like many others, lining their pockets with the aid of this
lucrative wartime traffic. They were incompetent drivers
too! Once our truck was slowly grinding its way uphill when
the driver carelessly cut a blind corner only to see another
truck full of passengers speeding downhill and heading
straight for us. Hoping to avoid a collision, the other truck
ploughed into the hillside, but the two trucks still met with

a tremendous impact. Everyone was badly shaken, but miraculously little real damage was done and no one was seriously hurt. Instead of the usual imprecations and re-criminations there was mutual congratulation on a very lucky escape. I told my companions how fortunate they were to be covered by the prayers of many people for my safety.

The ascent of the twenty-four hairpin bends followed, and from the top in the evening dusk we coasted down to yet another river, the last obstacle before Anshun. But torrential rain upstream had swollen the river to flood level, and as the storm broke over us the lightning revealed the truth: the pontoon bridge normally crossed during the hours of darkness because of its vulnerability to Japanese bombers, had broken up. It was to be many days before we could make the crossing. The small riverside town became hopelessly congested, and decent accommodation was impossible to find. Drivers and passengers gave themselves up to wine, women and mahjong. After three days, a man from the Chongqing Ministry of Foreign Affairs, hearing of my pres-ence in town, arranged for me to exchange my place in a miserable and evil hostelry for the comparative comfort of a camp bed in a truck drivers' dormitory at the China Travel Service hostel. A high-ranking Chinese military mission returning from staff talks with the British army in India, already overdue in Chongqing, was also marooned in the hostel. I found the general to be a Christian and that we had mutual friends in north China; a young subaltern in the party, a Sandhurst graduate, was also a Christian. Finding a telephone in the hostel, I actually got through to my wife in Anshun to explain the long delay. On the ninth day the military mission were at last able to leave, crossing the river on an improvised suspension bridge rigged up by the engineer in charge, but no one else was permitted to follow. When Paul Bartel of the Christian and Missionary Alliance caught us up, escorting four recently arrived CIM recruits, we heard on his radio the astounding news that Germany had declared war on Russia.

Eventually the waters of the Pan River subsided and the

pontoons were restored. Eleven days had already passed since arriving at this river crossing so, rather than wait for the truck, I decided to go on ahead with Bartel and his party in the station wagon. Passing two spectacular waterfalls we found ourselves in a region of conical limestone outcrops rising from the flat plain, like enormous wormcasts on a vast rippled beach, some of them tree-covered and with a temple at the top. In the fields, both Chinese and tribespeople were busy gathering in the harvest. A signpost marked "Anshun" directed us to a city with walls of white quarried stone and two picturesque rivers winding through it. The date was June 25th 1940, three months and three days after leaving Shanghai! Anshun was journey's end and home.

7 Miracle on the Burma Road (1940–44)

"Say among the nations, 'The Lord reigns!' . . .
He will judge the peoples with equity."

Psalm 96:10

Guizhou is one of the poorest provinces in China; it is also one of the wettest. The proverb says, "No three miles flat, no three days without rain and no three persons having an ounce of silver between them!" Hilly, wet and poor! The ever-changing mountain scenery made travel on foot or by bicycle a constant pleasure, in fine weather at least. The climate, however, was less attractive: it rained for most of the winter, a permanent "Scotch mist" making the paved streets slippery and dangerous. The summer weather was hot and often pleasant, but severe electric storms were frequent and sometimes terrifying. An early missionary had actually been killed by lightning in this city, an event which was regarded as a bad omen by the superstitious people he had come to help and which was consequently a serious setback for the work.

The poverty of the local people soon became evident, for Anshun, our home-to-be for four years, was a centre of the opium traffic; the fierce craving for the drug and runaway inflation were driving many of the city folk to crime. Our fellow missionaries regaled us with tales of men armed with knives climbing on to the verandahs of missionary residences to steal from the bedrooms whose occupants lay asleep. In our four years there thieves were constantly climbing over the surrounding compound wall to steal blankets, clothing, kitchenware or fruit from the trees. Even our washerwoman would regularly purloin items she fancied, even though they had been carefully counted out before and after she had washed them! Pickpockets operated on every street and at the weekly markets, while the police were totally incompetent and impotent. Guizhou was also very idolatrous, and Anshun seemed to be a city of spirit mediums whose eerie incantations in nearby houses often disturbed the silence of the nights. Our neighbours were indeed difficult to love!

A further drawback about life in Anshun was that it resembled Hamelin without a pied piper, being rat-infested to an appalling degree. Every household and shop owned a cat if it could afford one and, because cats were worth their weight in gold, kept the animal chained up by day. Even with a cat we could never rid our home of the resident rodents, which invaded our grain bins, had fun rolling potatoes down the stairs from our store and actually made their nests in our straw mattresses! This, then, was to be our future base of operations. Privation, poverty, severe and near-fatal illness, almost daily trials of faith and strong satanic opposition lay ahead. Anshun was to become for us a furnace of affliction and a valley of weeping, but, in the end, a place of fruitfulness.

The hospital staff consisted of Dr and Mrs Knight, old friends from Shanxi days, a lady doctor from Australia and two nurses from Australia and the USA. Our other colleagues were a Canadian couple responsible for the tribal work. The hospital was providing a much-needed and useful service to the community and the district; but, as we had been warned, the church itself had totally disintegrated. The last deacon had fallen a victim of opium and given up church-going. The huge church building stood empty and festooned with cobwebs; some services were, however, being maintained in the hospital chapel, mainly for patients.

The one mature Christian in the town was a medicine seller or self-styled "doctor" whose shop on the main street was faithfully closed on Sundays even when the day coincided with a market day when business would have been brisk. Dr Chen had, understandably, dissociated himself from the former congregation, but had maintained a family service in his own home; there he faithfully taught and catechised his wife and six children who, incidentally, formed a good choir. Soon after our arrival Dr Chen invited me to attend his family service, a perfect model of the "households of God" which would one day proliferate all over China. Our fellowship deepened, and we began to share a concern for the Lord's work in the city. Unlike most Chinese, who despised the tribal people from the mountains, Dr Chen always showed great sympathy for them and provided their chief medical care. Behind our own residence was a kind of barn where groups of Miao tribesmen (called "Hmong" in South-East Asia) visiting the city on business could stay overnight.

As I assumed responsibility for the English services in the hospital chapel I began to make friends with some of the doctors and students of the prestigious army medical college and the army veterinary college, and it soon became evident that an English Bible class would meet a need. This class was to become a main feature of our work, and among those who attended were people prominent in the medical and scientific world of China or who would one day become so. They included China's foremost pathologist (who also happened to be a direct descendant of Confucius) and other research scientists. The membership grew steadily to sixty in the first year, then to eighty and eventually to well over a hundred. At least a dozen people attended regularly during all the four years we were in Anshun, and there were clear conversions. One pharmacist, who later studied in England, is now Professor of Pharmacology at a certain university and a true Christian. Another married couple, both doctors, have continued to serve the Lord ever since those days, first opening a "Luke clinic" in China and later another in Macao before the husband entered the Baptist ministry in Hong Kong. It is inspiring to realise – and the fact must not be overlooked – that these doctors, veterinary surgeons and scientists who met regularly to study the Bible are today dispersed throughout China in key positions, some of them certainly maintaining their witness for Christ; others are active Christians in the USA. A sovereign God was manifestly preparing His witnesses among China's intellectuals both in Anshun and other west China cities for service in the Church of the future.

Among our possessions were a hand-wound gramophone and a good selection of classical records. As we were living in a culture-starved society, my suggestion to start a music club was greeted with enthusiasm. And so monthly meetings to listen to the music of Beethoven, Mozart or Tchaikovsky became very popular, a knowledgeable Chinese introducing the composers and the works to be played. This club served to break down barriers and to cement many friendships.

Within six months of our arrival, the invitations for which I had prayed began to materialise. First, the veterinary college invited me to lecture regularly on Christianity; then Dr C. P. Li, the director of the serum institute of the medical college invited me to teach English to a group of his research students. After dinner as the guest of Dr Li and his staff to meet General Chang, director of the medical college, I was asked by the general to become his English secretary.

Meanwhile, in Europe, the Germans were threatening Moscow and Stalingrad and carrying out heavy bombing raids on Britain. Rommel, however, was turned back from Egypt, and the Allies gained some notable naval victories in the Mediterranean. In China, the immediate fears were about a possible invasion of Burma by the Japanese and a consequent new threat from the west.

In Anshun we continued to plan for the future work of evangelism. We knew well that, once the war ended, all the "down-river" people from east China would return home. Since they could not, therefore, form a permanent nucleus of a local church, we began to give equal attention to reaching the local people. With Dr Chen's help we rented shop premises very near to the centre of the city and close to the ever popular theatre where the crowds gathered.

Cleaned up and decorated with colourful gospel posters, the open-fronted premises made a neat and attractive "preaching chapel". Every evening except on Saturdays and Sundays one or two Chinese Christians and I used to preach in rotation to the passing crowds for several hours on end. Some stayed for the whole time, while others listened just briefly. But over the years thousands heard the gospel, many fruitful contacts were made, numerous profitable private conversations with all sorts and conditions of men were held, quantities of Bibles were sold, follow-up visits were made to the villages, and some found Christ and were baptised.

Since Anshun was on the highway linking Chongqing with Kunming and Rangoon, travellers of all kinds were our constant visitors. The first very welcome guest was the Revd Marcus Cheng, the well-known Bible teacher and writer, who was on his way to Burma and Singapore but who stayed to be our delightful guest for a whole month. His visit was a golden opportunity to advertise a week of special meetings to be addressed by Marcus Cheng. Though the weather that autumn of 1940 was appalling, up to 150 people attended twice daily in the large chapel to hear very straightforward teaching on the Christian life, while 250 attended a special student service. This visit of God's servant was the first milestone on the road to recovery for the church in Anshun.

The highway also brought its tragedies. A young member of the Friends' Ambulance Unit who had died in the hospital from the all-too-prevalent typhus fever was buried in the Christian cemetery out among the hills. That year at least six of our fellow missionaries in Guizhou fell ill with this same disease. Then in February, Roland Hogben, the candidates' secretary in England, whom we had been expecting to visit us on his planned tour of China Inland Mission stations, had hardly started his journey when he was killed in a truck accident. Willie Windsor, our provincial superintendent, was also killed in a road accident and his body brought to Anshun to be laid to rest in the same cemetery. The heavy wartime losses among missionaries from disease and accident emphasised afresh the severe cost of missionary work.

Yet there were joys as well: during our time in Anshun two children were born to the Knights, and on March 22nd 1942 we welcomed our only son. Eggs and chickens and even a charming silver bracelet – typical gifts for such an event – arrived from all sources in celebration.

Following Marcus Cheng's meetings we decided to start holding regular services in the main chapel. November 23rd was a red-letter day when Dr Chen, who was now entering enthusiastically into the work as its virtual leader, attended with his whole family and himself preached the sermon. Christmas Eve was celebrated with a candlelight service in a packed chapel, and a large congregation gathered again on Christmas Day. We had been in Anshun for only six months.

On December 8th, following the Pearl Harbour disaster, the Allies had declared war on Japan, but Japan kept the initiative. First Thailand fell; then Malaya was invaded and Singapore lost. Manila, the capital of the Philippines, was captured, and both HMS *Repulse* and HMS *Prince of Wales*, Britain's capital ships, were sunk in the South China sea. Soon after, Hong Kong fell and Japanese forces invaded and finally occupied Burma right up to the Indian border. From Burma the Japanese crossed into China and, as frequent air-raid alarms disturbed our peace of mind, we and the Chinese began to feel threatened. Missionaries in every station actually discussed provisional evacuation plans. But the tide of war was turning: Rommel was defeated in north Africa and the Japanese fell back in Burma. The US Pacific fleet won the Battle of Midway, and Japan began to feel the weight of the first bombing raids on her own soil. But as the world's war ground on, the work in Anshun went forward encouragingly.

Bible classes in English and in Chinese, English classes in both colleges, the nightly evangelism at the street chapel and the Sunday services all produced a number of registrations for baptism, and special instruction classes were arranged. During the early months of 1941 attendances at all services increased and enthusiasm grew. In July the first

Daily Vacation Bible School for forty to fifty children was held and was followed up by the starting of a Sunday school which grew steadily as the year went by.

After the general had invited me to make a speech at the graduation ceremony of the army medical college, I was his guest at a party in the college gardens which were a glory of blossom and spring flowers. April 15th 1941 was our first Easter Day in Anshun. Already there was evidence of a resurrection in the church, for the dead bones were coming together and the wind of the Spirit was blowing. It had been the custom of local Christians to hold a picnic and a service at the Christian cemetery on Easter Day, and that year we joined them to celebrate the Saviour's victory over death. Later I spoke at the newly started Christian Endeavour class, and on April 18th thirty to forty Chinese friends attended a party in our garden. Then, to our joy, we received a letter from an itinerant evangelist saying that he had felt guided to come and minister in Anshun. Dr Chen and I therefore made arrangements for a series of meetings. Newman Shih's arrival marked the start of a long friendship which lasted until his death soon after visiting us in England in 1960. It also coincided with the desire expressed by many students and local people to be baptised: 150 were present to witness the confession of faith in baptism of the first twenty men and women, young and old. The following Sunday was a day to be remembered, as we celebrated the first Lord's Supper with seventy people taking part.

God was manifestly at work both among the students and professors as well as among the local citizens – but what about the tribespeople? Ill-health had taken the missionary family responsible for the tribes home to Canada, and this had left the additional responsibility for the oversight of the tribal churches on my shoulders. So that autumn Newman Shih and I set out for the two-day hike through wonderful mountain scenery to attend the annual church conference of the Big Flowery Miao tribe. God richly blessed the ministry of the Word, and the warmth of the welcome from those simple people was in striking contrast to the coldness we had first encountered in Anshun itself. But the weather was wintry, and, while sleeping on a couch of bracken was reasonably comfortable, two sweaters were needed to keep warm, even beneath a wadded Chinese quilt. Three hundred members of the church witnessed the baptism by immersion in the icy waters of a mountain stream of twenty-two young people. After a final meeting of praise and testimony, a large crowd escorted us over the hill on our way home.

Just as a living church was emerging in Anshun, a serious development occurred: another denomination appointed a pastor to open a second church in town. Knowing what confusion such a move was likely to cause in a city which had never known anything but one church, we immediately offered full co-operation. But this offer was coolly received and never followed up. Unfortunately the new arrival began to play the card of nationalism claiming that while the existing church was a "foreigners' church" his would be purely Chinese.

Meanwhile the economic situation had become quite desperate, for China was suffering from monumental inflation and prices were rising alarmingly. The central government, in order to accumulate foreign credits, had pegged the exchange rate of foreign currencies so that a donor's pound in England might be worth a shilling or less in purchasing power by the time it reached us; even then, that shilling would soon become worthless. So, on receiving our regular remittance from Chongqing, we immediately used it to purchase basic necessities. We also became very dependent on the sack of unpolished brown rice provided monthly by the medical college in return for my services. At times economic necessity forced us to sell our "luxuries": the carpets off the floor, a warm dressing-gown and any other non-essential possessions. We knew what it was to be poor, poorer far than local Chinese of our own station in life, and we had to trust God in a new way. The principle of faith in God in every circumstance, both on behalf of ourselves and our children, was put to a severe test.

Normally Westerners take butter, milk and sugar for

granted as everyday necessities, but in Anshun, butter was unavailable and the only sugar to be bought was in the form of brown blocks of very impure cane sugar which we had to refine ourselves. Since milk, especially for the children, was a necessity, the several missionary families owned cows or, as in our case, goats. Daily milking was a tiresome chore, but as the goats would be in milk for only six months in the year soya-bean milk had then to be used as a substitute for the rest of the year. The herdsman was an odd, totally unreliable tribesman, and on days when he failed to collect our goats I, like the prophet Amos, had to become a herdsman for the day, driving the goats out through the city gates to pasture, to the amazement of the guards and passers-by and all my normal activities had to be suspended for that day! There were other chores too: where such commonplace items as water-taps, plugholes and electric light switches were unheard of, much time and patience were needed to arrange baths in the family tin tub, to keep the sticky lumps burning vegetable oil lightworthy and in the daily emptying of the outside privy.

But against the background of world news and personal hardships God was showing us that the work was His responsibility by sending a lame ex-soldier to join us in the work as an evangelist, especially in connection with the street chapel, while his wife became our home help and cook. All kinds of people were now showing an interest in the gospel and coming for talks, so it was good to have a colleague with whom to pray daily and to share the ministry. Our second Christmas, when a large crowd attended an excellent programme of carols on Christmas Eve, was celebrated with even greater joy than before, and very early the following morning a carol party sang the Christmas message outside Christian homes in the city.

As the year 1942 ended, a church was again functioning, we had been joined by able fellow workers, Dr Chen and his family had become the backbone of the local Christian community, the tide of battle had turned and the prospects looked bright. But fiercer conflict lay ahead.

World War II began to go the way of the Allies in 1943 as the Germans were driven out of North Africa. The Allies landed in Sicily and then in Italy which soon dropped out of the war. The dam busters carried out their heroic mission, while the Ruhr was flooded and its industry crippled. But the cost of these victories was high. Victory in the spiritual warfare is also costly. When St. Paul said, "Death worketh in us but life in you," he was enunciating a fundamental principle of Christian service, namely that fruitfulness usually follows suffering; as one has said: "When we cease to bleed, we cease to bless." We were soon to experience in an acute way the working out of this principle in our own lives. It was to be in the fellowship of Christ's sufferings that we were to see the fruit of Christ's travail in Anshun. With St. Paul we could say: "I travail again in birth for you."

In January Andrew Gih, another of God's servants, who had visited Shanxi in 1931 with the Bethel Band, conducted a week of evangelistic meetings. Each evening the Christians held a torchlight procession to advertise the event, with the result that the chapel was filled to capacity twice daily to hear this powerful evangelist. Seventy signed decision forms, and in February we held a reception for the enquirers and started another instruction class. Spring returned, cheering us with flowers and fresh hope as Newman Shih announced his plan to return to Anshun on a permanent basis. On arrival he at once began a series of Bible studies in the Letter to the Ephesians, and then, judging that the time was ripe to push ahead with church organisation, called a meeting of the leading Christians at which fourteen persons were appointed to be church officers. One of their first responsibilities was to examine baptismal candidates, and, soon after, Easter Day was celebrated joyously with 180 people present to witness the dedication of the newly appointed leaders and twenty baptisms. The son of the famous "Christian general" Feng Yü-hsiang was among the sixty who attended the Holy Communion service. The new leaders took up their responsibilities conscientiously, and all arrangements for church affairs passed entirely into Chinese hands, a choir being formed and a church newspaper issued. We now welcomed Miss Chao, another experienced worker, to work among the women and to join our team of four which met every morning for united prayer.

Then the storm broke. First literally: the most violent night of thunder, lightning, rain and wind we ever experienced during our four years in Anshun kept us up all the night. A deafening thunder barrage and continuous flashing and flickering lightning turning night into day went on for hours. The gale-force winds blew the rain horizontally under the roof tiles into our upstairs rooms so that there was scarcely a dry spot anywhere and the water cascaded down the stairs like a waterfall. Clearing up the mess inside and outside the house took days. The city and the lovely gardens of the army medical college had suffered extensive damage. Then, with record numbers attending the weekly prayer meeting, some of us began to sense a coming satanic attack.

The attack took the form of a deliberate move to foment trouble between the two church congregations. A chance remark of mine had been misinterpreted as an insult, for which I was required to make a public apology before both congregations – a clear attempt to humiliate the foreigner. This affair was unpleasant enough, but a further trial was to follow when, on June 3rd, I became ill with a high temperature. The doctors diagnosed typhus fever, probably contracted when paying a regular visit to the local gaol to witness to the prisoners. Thanks to expert medical care and nursing I made a steady recovery. Professors, students and local Christians all showed great concern and true Christian kindness to the whole family during my illness. But the friction between the two congregations in the city was deeply disturbing, and Newman Shih, the main target of criticism by the other party, decided for the sake of peace to leave for the time being.

The spiritual conflict thickened when our elder daughter, then aged five, became ill with typhus and came to be nursed in the room adjoining mine. After days of high fever, the evening came when the doctor warned us that she might not live through the night. Instead of the deep distress which one would expect, after we had committed the child into God's hands I was given "the garment of praise for the spirit of heaviness", almost a feeling of elation, and received the definite assurance that she would be preserved to us. Though she survived the night, to our joy and relief, our faith was tested for a further fifteen days as the patient's temperature continued to fluctuate, bringing increasing strain on the heart, before the crisis finally ended and the two of us could convalesce together. All God's waves and billows had swept over us, but now there was calm.

As soon as the doctor permitted, I gladly rejoined the daily prayer meeting, now augmented by "Timothy" Chang, one of the Christian students who had dropped out of his medical course. A short mission led by two members of the Bethel Band gave the church a further impetus and that summer nearly sixty children attended a second Daily Vacation Bible School. Even firing outside the city and the imposition of martial law failed to interrupt the programme. By now, the whole family, after the long weeks of illness, strain and anxiety, needed a break.

Zunyi, further along the highway, is famous for having staged the historic conference in 1937, at which Mao Zedong, during the Long March, had assumed supreme power within the Party and finally rejected the tutelage of Stalin. Knowing our need for a change, our colleagues in Zunyi had invited us to visit them for a short holiday. We spent the time sightseeing, picnicking, swimming in the river, climbing the surrounding hills, attending a local sports meeting and celebrating the Mid-Autumn Festival, moon cakes and all, with Christian students from the local refugee university. I even addressed the military foreign language school on the subject of "A typical English family"! We returned home refreshed and to be present when sixteen more converts were welcomed into the church fellowship. A newly arrived doctor, a Scot, joined me on my annual visit to the tribal conference in the mountains, and Dave grudgingly agreed that the scenery was comparable to the Scottish Highlands! While Dave treated patients I gave the addresses at the conference meetings, and, on the misty hillside, we witnessed further baptisms.

Newman Shih eventually returned to Anshun, and we became especially conscious of God's presence at our workers' prayer meetings. As another Christmas came, the chapel was splendidly decorated and again large numbers attended the carol service. Then at the time of the Chinese New Year Dr Chen invited the church leaders and ourselves to a splendid feast at his home, a wonderful occasion of joy and fellowship. Little did we then suspect that within ten years all these fine Christian people would be enduring severe tests of their faith under a Communist government, but God was already preparing them for this very thing.

In 1944, the Allies landed in Europe on their victorious way to the Rhine. In China, however, it was a different story for resistance to the Japanese was crumbling. The highway suddenly became busier than ever as American trucks and "jeeps" (then a novelty) transported personnel and armaments to front-line air bases east of us, hoping to stem further Japanese advances. The British Military Mission (BMM) also became more active, and we entertained a VIP party including Sir Hugh Prideaux Bruce, the British chargé d'affaires. Another distinguished guest who stayed in our home for a week was the Cambridge scientist and sinologue Dr Joseph Needham, for whom I interpreted at a reception in the medical college. When the Chinese armies proved incapable of providing support for the US air force, long convoys of Americans began moving back in the opposite direction. Kind GIs passing through unloaded on us powdered milk, ice-cream mix, butter, cocoa and coffee – luxuries unheard of by the children and half-forgotten even by ourselves: a "table in the wilderness" indeed!

Our fourth year in Anshun began well when three leading Chinese Christians, Calvin Chao, founder of the China Inter-Varsity Fellowship, Dr Yen and Paul Shen, held a week of meetings for both Christians and non-Christians;

many more received Christ and gave stirring testimonies to
the fact. After Newman Shih had conducted the first baptisms of the year, "Timothy" Chang and I set out again for
the mountains to hold Bible classes for tribal Christians.
The weather was appalling, and the carrier complained
about his load. After missing our way several times in the
fog and rain, we finally arrived, tired and mud-stained.
While messengers went out to call the people in, I did
some visiting in local homes and was shocked by the stark
simplicity of the tribal life-style. The cold was intense, icicles
hung from the eaves of the huts and the trees were encrusted
with ice. But even a snowfall did not prevent thirty people
from attending worship on Sunday when I began a series of
talks on Exodus for men and youths, while Timothy was the
preacher each evening. As the Holy Spirit moved in hearts,
earnest prayers for God's forgiveness accompanied tears of
repentance. Our small leaders' groups consisting of tribal
leaders, a Chinese student and a foreigner enjoyed an unforgettable few days of prayer and fellowship when, as our
hearts were melted together, we became totally oblivious of
the differences between us of race, culture and nationality;
the consciousness of our complete oneness in Christ and of
Christ in our midst was a peak experience for us all and one
we can never forget.

It was during this visit that I heard more of the story of
the past work among this particular tribe. As is normally
the case among tribal animists, there had in the past been
a mass turning from spirit worship to Christianity, but it
was left to a young Welshman to lead individuals to repentance from sin before they had begun to experience new life
in Christ. The real Christian leaders in the tribe were those
who had come into a living and saving faith through this
young missionary's ministry, brief though it had been on
account of ill health. Reluctantly Timothy and I bid farewell
to our tribal friends, who had shown us such warm hospitality, and left the icy heights. The tribal Christians in that
area were to have no further ministry from missionaries
before the Communist take-over ten years later. Like their

brethren elsewhere this church, too, would experience persecution and suffering for Christ's sake.

The day after our return, following thirty days of ceaseless rain, the sun shone for the first time and the Chinese New Year was celebrated in the usual cheerful fashion. But events were moving fast. Locally, it had been decided to transfer the missionary personnel of the hospital to Dali to augment the staff of the hospital there and to sell the hospital premises to the medical college. We said goodbye to our medical friends, and I accepted an invitation to take part in a student conference in Sichuan. This took me on the long journey to Chongqing by BMM truck. After an excellent student conference I visited the Holy Light School, started by a provincial treasurer for the children of government officials and also Dr Chia Yuming's Bible school in the Chongqing hills. While I was in that area Christians in the Ministry of Education invited me to take up work among them, and since our goal of an autonomous church in Anshun seemed near to achievement the invitation held a strong attraction.

I returned to Anshun in time to welcome Paul Shen, an earlier visitor, whom the church committee had invited to become their pastor. Paul received an enthusiastic reception from the congregation and at once took full responsibility for all church meetings, setting us completely free to contemplate the move to Chongqing. In September there arrived the moment which all missionaries dread: the first break in the family circle when their child goes away to boarding school. A few days before she was due to leave, a thief stole her entire outfit which had taken months to prepare! After escorting our elder daughter to her school in Sichuan, I attended three days of council meetings of the China Inland Mission in Chongqing. It was thrilling to hear how, all over "free China", God was at work in ways similar to those in Anshun: students were turning to Christ in their hundreds, new churches were being planted and old established ones revived. At those meetings, too, policies were formulated for the guidance of the work of the Mission in a post-war situation. Bishop Houghton took Ephesians 3:10 as the essential principle for the future: the work of the Mission would, henceforth, be "through the church", the Mission members channelling their gifts through the local churches in which they would function as full members. Finally, our proposed move to the new sphere in Chongqing with the Ministry of Education was formally approved and I returned to Anshun to announce this decision to the church. A week of well-attended evangelistic meetings followed and we witnessed the baptism of another twenty-seven persons and shared with the church the encouragement when a US navy man donated US $1,000 for the work. My wife and I then took our last Bible classes, and after being fêted by our friends we joined a BMM convoy en route to Chongqing.

As we said goodbye to our Anshun brethren we felt deeply moved. We had arrived to find a defunct church, and now we were leaving behind a vigorous and united congregation having a membership of well over 100 with able leadership and a fine young pastor in charge. All the travail had been worth while, and we had been privileged to see God perform a miracle on the Burma road. That miracle was one of many similar miracles taking place in west China which would make a vital contribution to the upbuilding of the Church in the post-war China. Careful Bible students have noted that the "seed" in the two parables of the sower and the tares is not the same: in the one it is the Word of God, while in the other it is "the sons of the kingdom" (Matthew 13:38, RSV) or the embodied Word. So in Anshun not only had the seed of God's Word been sown in many hearts, producing a harvest, but the good seed of the "sons of the kingdom" would eventually be scattered broadcast in every province of China – as doctors, chemists, consultants, lecturers, research scientists and the like. The seed may die, but if it dies it brings forth an abundant harvest. The world is now witnessing the truth of this principle in the multiplying millions of Christians in China.

8 God Can Be Trusted! (1946)

"The Lord reigns; let the people tremble! He sits
enthroned . . . let the earth quake!"

Psalm 99:1

Our journey to Sichuan ended abruptly. We had completed
the first stage to Guiyang, the provincial capital, when a
sudden Japanese thrust in December 1944 seemed to
threaten not only Guiyang but also Chongqing itself. The
British embassy had advised the evacuation of its nationals
as a matter of urgency, and our BMM convoy was given
instructions to turn around and head for Kunming, four
days' journey away. Within hours we had disposed of
surplus possessions which could not be taken out of China.
Our "flight" in open trucks was in the winter and, with
Christmas near and ice and snow covering the higher
mountain passes near to our destination, it seemed appropriate to keep up our spirits by singing such carols as
"In the Bleak Midwinter".

Formalities in Kunming were quickly completed, and
with little delay we found ourselves, as if on a magic carpet,
in an RAF plane flying over "the hump" en route to Calcutta. The children needed oxygen at the highest altitude
over the southern section of the Himalayas, but once we
were back on the ground and in the officers' mess at Dum
Dum Airport their sleepy eyes opened wide at the sight of
tall Indian servants wearing turbans and red cummerbunds
waiting on them at the dinner table! More wonders still
were in store: electric light, running water, flush toilets,

buses, Western-style stores and a cinema showing *Snow White
and the Seven Dwarfs*!

Our eldest child, who had been at school in Sichuan, was
still missing from the family circle. With a planeload of other
children she had taken off from a Sichuan airfield in an
American evacuation plane bound for Kunming; but, an air
raid being in progress, the pilot had made for an alternative
airstrip; then, losing his bearings in the clouds, he had flown
round and round searching in vain for a place to land.
Suddenly, a break in the clouds had revealed the very
airstrip for which he had been looking and, with a nearly
empty fuel tank, he had made a safe landing. The pilot had
been a vastly relieved man! Needless to say, we too gave
thanks to God when we heard the story. After this seven-
year-old had flown on to Calcutta, our family was complete
and we were accommodated in a missionary home. When
Christmas Day came, the children were delighted to share
the traditional celebration around the tree with a family of
Indian children for a change.

After several weeks delay in Calcutta when we did some
necessary shopping and explored the city, we crossed the
subcontinent to Bombay by train to await transport back to
England. Again, the delay had its delights – the Breach
Candy swimming club and the zoo – but when it dragged
on for several months, I pleaded the urgent need for my
services in my stepfather's school. My plea was successful,
and we were given a first class passage on a liner largely
reserved for senior army personnel. Carrying our life belts
wherever we went on board, we crossed the Indian Ocean
safely, passed through the Suez Canal, and sailed peacefully
through the Mediterranean to Gibraltar. There we joined a
large, well-protected convoy for the last stage of the voyage
to Liverpool. En route, by request, I lectured on China to
a mixed audience of senior officers, the governor of Aden
and some naval ratings. This lecture led to interesting conversations, but considerable scepticism was expressed about
my prediction that China would eventually fall to the Communists.

The family warmly welcomed us home to Hoylake in Cheshire, where I quickly took up teaching small boys again. Among my pupils was a very bright twelve-year-old called Fred. A postcard written in 1980, in reply to a letter I had addressed to the MEP Sir Frederick Catherwood following his visit to China, said briefly: "No need to introduce yourself. We met when I wore short trousers!" VE and VJ days were celebrated thankfully and joyously. Then in May a third daughter arrived to complete our family.

It was not easy to contemplate taking our four children back to a war-torn China, but our sense of call to that land remained strong. There were still no scheduled transatlantic shipping services, so when we were unexpectedly warned of a ship about to call at Liverpool we had only forty-eight hours to prepare! The *Gripsholm* had been a prisoner-exchange ship during the war. The voyage to New York was uneventful and, after quarantine in Philadelphia for whooping cough, we moved on to Vancouver. Due to the unexpected delay, and after we had freighted our heavy baggage out of Vancouver to Shanghai, the money in our bank account was exhausted; having purchased a few small necessities and with the long journey to China ahead of us, we were exactly penniless! Here was a fresh test of the principles by which we had lived ever since joining the China Inland Mission. We were to travel south by train to San Francisco, where we would join other missionaries on the *Marine Lynx*, a US troop ship bound for Shanghai. On December 8th we made a final call on my wife's parents to say goodbye. My father-in-law had just been handed ten dollars and, knowing nothing of our financial plight, he passed this gift on to us as we left for the railway station. There, someone else pressed a five-dollar note into my hand; and fifteen dollars was just sufficient to meet the cost of our meals during the two days' and nights' journey.

On arrival in San Francisco, I found awaiting me an invitation to speak at a Bible school in Oakland. After the meeting I was handed the free-will offering of $9.48, which proved to be precisely the amount needed to transport the family cases to the docks. As we waited for the day of embarkation, kind friends entertained us and showed us around that fascinating city. Two further gifts totalling six dollars covered incidental expenses for the children, including a real American ice-cream! When we left the house of our host, our purse was again empty and we were embarrassed to be unable to pay the modest ten dollars suggested for the board. At the station, however, two people handed me five-dollar notes, and so, even as we queued for the train, I was able to pass the ten dollars to our kind friend through the barrier which separated us. As we boarded the ship which was to carry 300 missionaries back to China our pockets were once more empty, and we were to spend Christmas at sea. Other passengers would have access to the well-stocked navy shop (or PX), but that would not be for us! So imagine our delight to find on board, addressed to "the Lyalls", a huge hamper of Christmas luxuries ordered by an old friend in Buffalo, in the eastern United States! All the way to China we lacked no good thing and Christmas was celebrated in style.

Accommodation for the passengers was in two huge holds, one for the men and the other for the women. There were long rows of three-tier canvas berths and no privacy whatever. As Christmas approached gay little Christmas trees surprisingly appeared by each family section. Among the passengers were Dr Fenn, known to all missionaries as the compiler of a Chinese–English dictionary, who offered classes in Chinese for the new recruits who included Arthur Glasser, a future OMF director and well-known missiologist There were also several "Navigator" missionaries and representatives of the Pocket Testament League as newcomers among the old-timers, all eager to take advantage of the post-war opportunities to evangelise China. An early Communist take-over was far from our thoughts; indeed, optimism was strong among everyone on board.

Whooping cough was past, but in Vancouver mumps had been going the rounds with the result that our children began to develop the symptoms and one of them had to go into the sick bay. We had received so many tokens of God's provision for us that we were a little surprised to receive yet another five dollars: we discovered the reason when the sick-bay attendant asked us for just that amount in payment for services rendered. So penniless we had set out and penniless we arrived in Shanghai, yet in between every need had been met by a faithful God.

During the war the CIM buildings in Shanghai had been commandeered by the Japanese army as their headquarters. After their surrender in 1945, the premises were recovered. Unheated though they were, the Japanese having torn out the heating system for scrap metal, 1531 Sinza Road became a real home away from home for our family. It was many weeks before mumps and finally chicken-pox had taken their full courses with each of the four children. Quarantine proved to be a long, tedious process: first in Philadelphia, then in Vancouver and last of all in Shanghai.

The delay gave me the opportunity to take part in a student conference in Nanjing, the capital, where I renewed acquaintance with Dr C. P. Li (of Anshun days) and his family. Dr Li was soon to gain distinction in the scientific world of the USA. Back in Shanghai we received a welcome back from other Anshun friends, including my former boss the general, the pathologist descendant of Confucius and "Timothy" Chang, who was now the general secretary of the China Inter-Varsity Fellowship, a position which was to involve him in serious trouble with the Communist authorities and years of suffering until his rehabilitation in 1979. Calvin Chao, the founder of the China IVF, also came to discuss student work. It was a special joy to be welcomed by David Yang, who was then living in Shanghai and dividing his time between pastoring churches there and in Nanjing. The wedding of my wife's Chinese bridesmaid, Ruth Wang, was a highlight of those days. Ruth was the senior consultant at the prestige Margaret Williamson Hospital, Shanghai. Her husband was a leading industrialist and, as it later appeared, a personal friend of Zhou Enlai, the future premier of China, though not himself a Communist. In 1982 Ruth, with whom we have tried to keep contact, would be honoured in Peking as one of China's "Two hundred distinguished women".

At last the long delay came to an end, and we began to make plans to go north again to Peking, where Christian students had invited us to be their advisers. David Adeney had already spent a short time in Peking following up student contacts there before taking up his responsibilities among students in Shanghai. Other CIM members had been invited to university centres in Nanjing, Chengdu, Chongqing, Lanzhou and elsewhere. Our hopes and expectations were high. Little did we realise how short our opportunity would be! The year was 1946, and by 1949 Communism would have triumphed. In 1951 missionaries would be on their way out of China once more – this time finally!

9 Student Revival in Peking (1946–48)

"Hallelujah! For the Lord our God the Almighty reigns."

Revelation 19:6

In 1947, travel in China was still far from normal and the only available passenger transport to Tientsin was by a wartime LST (Landing Ship Tank). Leaving the two older girls behind in Shanghai to attend school, my wife and I and our two younger children boarded this vessel in which men, women and children all occupied the same crew quarters and used the same bathroom facilities. Once more, for the next ten days, there was to be no privacy; there was no safety on deck either, because this was no passenger ship and precautions against children falling overboard were non-existent. So most of the time was spent sitting, lying or playing on our bunks in full view of all the other passengers: English, American, Chinese, Russian, etc. Interesting conversations with some of the passengers helped to pass the time, including a discussion on Communism with a Russian Jew.

After a stormy day or two, our ship docked at Qingdao, the former German port, on March 11th. The distant rumble of artillery fire made us aware that the civil war, which had resumed after the end of hostilities with Japan, was again raging. It was March 16th before we reached Taku Bar, too late to cross until the following day. The north China weather was bitterly cold and it was a relief to arrive, tired and travel-worn, at the comfortable CIM home in Tientsin, where before the war we had often had fellowship with Eric Liddell, the hero of the recent Oscar-winning film *Chariots of Fire*. Leaving the family to recover, I set off for Peking with my all-essential bicycle, my objective being to find a home in what was already an overcrowded city. Since VJ Day the sixty million refugees, including thousands of university students, had been pouring back from west China to the cities in the east.

Peking, many have claimed, shares with Paris the distinction of having been the most beautiful city in the world. We soon discovered the elusive charm of this majestic, ancient and historic former capital of China to be as inescapable as it was difficult to analyse and describe. Its massive walls, pierced by eight huge and impressive gates, the vast former palace of the emperors and empresses, with its roofs of golden tiles shining in the sun, known as the "Forbidden City", the dignified Temple of Heaven and the associated Altar of Heaven, the charming palace lakes, the exquisite Summer Palace and lake and the infinite variety of beauty in the Western Hills made Peking a city utterly unique. Designed by Kublai Khan in the thirteenth century, it had changed little in 600 years and now encapsulated the colourful history and magnificent culture of Chinese civilisation. All too soon profound changes would occur when it would become the capital of a new empire, a Communist empire, and the seat of a new "emperor", Mao Zedong. The ancient walls would be torn down, all but two of the magnificent gates would disappear, and huge construction schemes extending in all directions would remove the old landmarks and transform the city into a strictly functional capital. Only the Forbidden City, with its associated lakes and parks, would be preserved and renovated as monuments to the great artistry and skills of which Chinese workers had been capable in the past and which were presented as a challenge to workers of a new generation to emulate. We were privileged to live in and enjoy old Peking in its twilight years.

Seven or eight missionary societies were at work there, but the largest single congregation was that of the independent church known as the Christian Tabernacle, of which Mr Wang Mingdao was the pastor. As I arrived, the city was in the midst of the notorious seasonal dust storms, when choking yellow loess blew in clouds straight from the Gobi Desert. Most cyclists wore gauze masks by way of protection. Day by day I pursued my almost hopeless search for a house, while on most evenings I accepted invitations to speak to groups of students.

After ten days of fruitless search with no suitable house in sight, I went to morning worship at the Tabernacle rather discouraged. After the service a lady, a complete stranger, approached me: "Mr Lyall, I believe that you are looking for a house for your work, I have one for rent which might suit you. Would you like to come and see it?"

Eagerly I accepted the invitation, and together we arrived outside No. 33 Hsi Tsung Pu Hutung (an address soon to be on the lips of many!). Tall red lacquered pillars stood on either side of a massive black gate with steps leading up to a porch graced by pots of oleander and leading into a charming front courtyard overlooked by graceful latticed windows. The room between the front and back courtyards was a huge guest hall capable of seating 200 people. It had once been a showroom for Peking carpets where world tourists came to make their costly purchases. Black lacquered pillars lined the hall and beautifully carved horn lanterns hung from the ceiling. The spacious living quarters lay beyond, and of course there was running water, electricity and even central heating, luxuries we had never before enjoyed during our twenty years in China. "No. 33" was a typical Peking residence of the wealthy, so palatial that it took my breath away. It had even been the temporary home of General Marshall's deputy when he was attempting – as it proved, in vain – to arrange a truce in the disastrous civil war between the Nationalists and the Communists. Could such a magnificent place be meant for poor missionaries like ourselves? The usual bargaining over rent began, and telegrams flew backwards and forwards between us and the CIM Headquarters in Shanghai. Agreement was finally reached on a quite absurd rental for such a splendid Peking mansion; but as Mrs Li, the owner, said, it was for the Lord's work. For what work, I was bound to ask myself? How could we justify living in such oriental splendour? Time would soon show!

On April 21st, as lilacs, wisteria and peonies graced the lovely Peking parks, our family moved into "No. 33", where we were joined by a wonderful cook who could rise to any occasion, whether preparing a big wedding breakfast or catering for fifty or more students at a conference. An American lady colleague with experience of student work in the north-west now joined us, and we began to pray together about God's plan for the days ahead. As soon as it was known where we lived a stream of visitors, Chinese and foreign, called to see us, and on May 1st fifteen missionaries of various societies shared a house-warming tea. They at once decided to hold an English service on Sunday evenings in our guest room, a regular weekly prayer meeting and a Sunday school for our children, activities which flourished with thirty or more regularly attending the weekly service in English.

It was not long before I received invitations to hold Bible classes in four of Peking's universities: Peking, Tsinghua, Yenching and Fu Ren (Roman Catholic) as well as in some of the other fifteen colleges. These classes necessitated long, almost daily journeys by bicycle in all weathers: the intense heat of summer and the equally intense cold of winter. Christian students in the various colleges who had so recently returned to their own campuses had not yet met one another, and when I told the groups about the others, they asked: "Where can we get together?" "Well, we are now living in the east city," I replied. "How about coming to see us?"

When a group of students arrived at No. 33, they were as astounded as we had been by God's amazing provision and promptly adopted the place as their headquarters. They decided to hold a monthly gathering in the guest hall at eight o'clock on Sunday morning before church. It was a small beginning!

One member of the Yenching Bible class was obviously a born leader, and "Peter" soon took control. When numbers at this monthly meeting grew we decided to make it a weekly event, the students, poor though they were, subscribing to buy additional simple benches needed for increased seating accommodation. The Spirit of God was clearly moving.

One of the students' first ventures was the publication of a *Gospel Magazine* which was launched with great enthusiasm but against the background of high political tension. On May 20th, on my way to Fu Ren, I met a procession of student demonstrators carrying banners with slogans such as "End the civil war!" and "End our empty stomachs!" Educational grants were a mere pittance, and students had to exist on the sparsest of fare, basically maize buns. The Nationalist government had forfeited all confidence, and newspapers reported constant student demonstrations and some bloodshed. A train was derailed by Communist guerillas near Peking, causing over 100 casualties. While Communist activities were reported all around the city a local curfew was imposed. In Manchuria, the Nationalist forces were suffering defeat after defeat. Within every Peking college, Communist cells were intensifying indoctrination among their members.

In spite of the tense political situation, the Christian student committee went ahead with arranging a conference in August following the IVF National Conference in July. The Peking delegation of four to that conference in Nanjing, two men and two women, found several hundred other students gathered representing every university in China, the majority of them aflame with their first love for Christ. Others were comparative veterans, having been converted during the war and some having attended the only previous evangelical student conference in Chongqing in 1943. Our missionary colleagues from all over China were there, and we joyfully shared the thrilling news of what God was doing in the student world.

At the opening ceremony each group, including our own, introduced itself and sang a song. Every morning, groups under experienced leaders met for Bible reading and prayer. The speakers – Calvin Chao, David Yang, Andrew Gih, Dr Chia Yüming and several foreigners, including Bishop Houghton – were dynamic. One day Madame Chiang Kai-shek visited the conference to bring a message of welcome from the President. Everyone was fully aware of the gravity of the national situation, and as these young people sought God for His blessing, both for themselves as individuals and for the nation as a whole, the spiritual temperature rose daily. Those were tremendous days, the like of which would never be repeated, though forty years later the memory lives on. All these young people were soon to be confronted with the choice of "Christ or Communism?", and all who chose Christ would be called to suffer greatly for His sake. Our delegation returned to Peking full of new enthusiasm and on the return journey by sea freely witnessed for Christ to fellow passengers.

The Peking committee now held frequent meetings to plan for their own conference, the venue of which was to be an orphanage adjoining the lovely grounds of the Summer Palace. The preparatory organisation was excellent, nothing being overlooked; and at last, on August 16th, trucks transported 120 students to the site. Seeing that students were so desperately poor the organisers had agreed to make no charge for board: whatever cash was placed in the free-will offering box on any one day would be used to buy provisions for the following day – a practice which left no one hungry!

The speakers were David Yang and Wang Mingdao, the latter preaching daily on sin and the former on the glory of Christ. Deep conviction was soon manifested and as individuals repented they experienced the joy of forgiveness. One husky physical training student, during a quite un-emotional meeting, suddenly began sobbing, and a counsellor took him aside and led him to Christ. Many were clearly converted, while those already Christians entered more deeply into the fullness of salvation. The student leaders had no patience at any time with mere superficial profession, baptism and church membership in their eyes counting for nothing in themselves. The sole criterion was "Has he life?", meaning new life from God, the "life of God in the soul of man" resulting from the new birth of the Spirit. Of every convert it was always asked "Has he life?" or "Has she life?" The tide of spiritual blessing rose daily, and the final testimony meeting brought the conference to a mighty climax. We had witnessed and experienced a moving of the Spirit – a true reviving – as God had answered prayer beyond all our expectations.

The trucks carrying the students back to their campuses drove along Chang An Street, which today is the ceremonial route past the Tien An Men (Gate of Heavenly Peace) where loud shouts of praise for Chairman Mao have often been heard. But in 1947 the students were singing joyful songs of praise to God; and Peking, which has always been the spearhead of student revolution in China, had never seen or heard the like before.

But life in Peking did not revolve entirely around the student work. One day a young air force officer called at No. 33. He turned out to be one of Gladys Aylward's orphans and later brought a friend who was not yet a Christian, to introduce her to my wife. Would she teach the girl, please? Of course! And before their wedding in our guest hall the girl became, and has remained, a very stalwart Christian. This couple escaped with the Nationalist armies to Taiwan where Tien, the husband, rose to the rank of colonel and became a prominent leader in Watchman Nee's assemblies.

When rest and respite were needed, Peking provided lovely places for retreat. That autumn we enjoyed a few days at a temple in the Western Hills amid splendid scenery before returning to face the urgent demands of the work: daily Bible classes which were preparing splendid young people for a future under Communism; the chairmanship of the Peking Youth for Christ and its plans for even wider evangelism; frequent preaching engagements and a weekly gospel radio broadcast. Meanwhile the student leaders were preparing a constitution for the Fellowship and wisely decided against affiliation with the China IVF, so enabling the Peking Fellowship to survive for four years after the national organisation had been compelled by the Communist authorities to disband.

But the students were facing problems: Satan could not allow this powerful work of the Holy Spirit to go unchallenged. Issues of modernist biblical interpretation raised by the SCM kept arising, and some groups were threatened by division, for it was impossible in a city like Peking to avoid extremes of teaching on the subject of the Holy Spirit. Fortunately most of the students attended the Tabernacle, where they were sure to be nourished on sound doctrine. On November 28th, in spite of the failure of the central heating at No. 33, a record crowd of students jammed into all the available space and, through snow and ice, they continued to come, some from long distances.

In the current political atmosphere students found themselves living in two worlds: the world of Christian fellowship and that of Communist propaganda. At one leaders' meeting "Peter" suggested following the well-known practice followed in Communist cells, of self-criticism and mutual criticism. At first the experiment when transposed into Christian terms was quite successful, reminiscent as it was of the old Oxford Group practice of honest "sharing"; but at subsequent meetings the criticism tended to fall short of what was loving and sometimes became unkind. Members were hurt unnecessarily, and the practice was abandoned.

The Student Fellowship constantly welcomed visiting speakers such as Andrew Lu of the Pocket Testament League, Bob Pierce of Youth for Christ and Dawson Trotman, founder of the Navigators, who gave a powerful message to a record audience of 200. All such speakers were making a valuable contribution to the strengthening of the growing student movement throughout China.

Meanwhile the civil war was going badly for the government: city after city in north China fell to the well-disciplined, well-equipped Communist armies as the Nationalist forces became increasingly demoralised. Refugees flocked to Peking, and we ourselves entertained one old lady from a wealthy peasant family who had lost everything, and yet she never ceased to testify: "I still have the Lord!" He was her real and lasting inheritance. There were thousands like her.

January 1948 turned bitterly cold when, for ten days, the guest hall was crowded for a winter conference. As many as fifty shared a noon meal, and some of the leaders were our house guests for the whole time. "Peter" and I were the main speakers, though Wang Mingdao also spoke once or twice. As numbers increased, so did the evidence of God's blessing. Between the sessions every room in the house, including our bedroom, was full of praying groups. These young people knew something of what to expect under Communist rule and had a consuming desire to know God in such a way that their faith would not fail. The long and heart-warming final testimony meeting showed that God had been present in power.

Throughout 1948 attendance at the Sunday morning meeting varied from 100 to 200. During the Chinese New Year holiday different college groups held fellowship meetings in the guest hall and committees of various kinds met there too, including one to organise New Year open-air witness bands. These were well supported, and the students, mostly new to open-air preaching, gained in boldness and confidence each day. Despite snow and sleet the bands continued their witness in different areas of the city and suburbs. Easter followed when a fleet of trucks took about 200 students out for a day's retreat at the Bible school in the Western Hills whose principals, two fine women called Miss Pi and Miss Liu, gave stirring addresses. We all paid a respectful visit to the nearby tomb of Dr John Sung, the well-known and widely loved scholar-evangelist and Bible teacher whose ministry had contributed so greatly to the

transformation of the life of the Church in China and its
preparation for the trials to come.

Politically, China was nearing the end of an era. In June,
student strikes and demonstrations again erupted in Peking
to protest against government failures and American aid to
Japan. Then in July, the sound of gunfire just ten miles
away was clearly heard and the railway line to Tientsin was
blown up by Communist guerilas. University classes had
come to an end in mid-June, setting me free to give more
time to the affairs of Youth for Christ.

The committee had decided to stage a city-wide evangelistic campaign and had sent invitations to Andrew Gih and
Bob Pierce to be the missioners. With police permission, a
large auditorium of which the surrounding walls and the
covering over the stand were made of straw matting was
erected on the polo ground adjoining the historic Legation
Quarter where in 1900 the Boxer soldiers had besieged the
foreign community. Electric lights and loudspeakers were
installed, but owing to their failure on the opening night
and the non-arrival of Bob Pierce the mission got off to a
bad start. The second meeting, however, created a deep
impression, and at the end of it large numbers came to the
front, over 120 of whom returned the following evening to
pray. Every day, eighty or ninety arrived early for counsel-
ling and prayer *before* the main meeting.

Day temperatures soared into the hundreds, and some of
the workers found the heat exhausting; but except for one
windy, dusty evening large crowds continued to listen to
the gospel simply and powerfully proclaimed. Scores were
counselled daily and, as the campaign ended, about 100
enquirers responded to the invitation to come for consecutive
teaching at No. 33, over eighty of whom faithfully attended
the whole series. This city-wide mission was without doubt
the first of its kind ever to have been held in the city's
history. It was certainly the largest and proved to be the
final attempt before the city fell to the Communists to reach
the Peking masses with the gospel.

In addition to the many well-known foreign mission or-

ganisations in Peking with their fine hospitals and schools
– the American Presbyterians and the Methodists in particular – there were also some comparatively unknown
Chinese servants of God who were faithfully making Christ
known. In the "Chinese city" outside the towering walls of
the imperial "Tartar city", for example, a young preacher
and his wife who were childless were shepherding a congregation of poor working-class people. Their only living-room
was the bare chapel itself where, among the pews, they ate
their meals, the wife worked with her sewing-machine and
the "pastor" kept his bicycle. The only privacy they enjoyed
was in the small "vestry" which doubled as their bedroom.
But, as God honoured the preaching of His Word, the
small chapel became too small to accommodate the growing
congregation and an extension to the chapel became essential. Yet how could the money for this purpose be found?
The pastor and his wife possessed only three items of saleable
value: a sewing-machine, a bicycle and a wrist-watch. The
sewing-machine was essential to their livelihood. A watch,
too, is essential for every preacher – if he looks at it! That
left the bicycle; after all, the pastor could walk instead of ride
on his pastoral visits. So the two agreed to sell the bicycle
and, because inflation quickly devalued cash, they immediately bought as many sacks of flour as the proceeds permitted
and piled them up in the chapel. When the worshippers
arrived on the following Sunday and saw the sacks of flour
they were so moved by this sacrificial act that they all made
sacrifices of their own, and each added his or her own
contribution to the flour pile until the proceeds of the sale
of the flour met the cost of the needed extension. It was
always a joy to worship with such people, whose love for
Christ and for one another overflowed in sacrificial giving.
And it would be sacrificial giving of this kind that would
ensure genuine "self-support" among the household
churches of the future.

Meanwhile attendance at the Sunday fellowship at No.
33 continued to crowd the guest hall, and a spirit of serious-
ness and earnestness characterised every meeting. The mess-

age of 1 Peter which had prepared the Church of the first
century for imminent suffering was solemnly received; its
teaching on Christian foundations, the nature of the living
Church, the ethical witness of Christians under persecution
and the privilege of suffering for Christ was acutely relevant
to their present situation: "Beloved, do not be surprised at
the fiery ordeal which comes upon you to prove you as
though something strange were happening to you. But rejoice in so far as you share Christ's sufferings, that you may
also rejoice and be glad when His glory is revealed." Many
who listened to those expositions would, not many years
later, be plunged into prolonged suffering and survive to
testify that suffering had been something they had been
privileged to bear for Christ. Others may well have died for
their faithfulness.

In that summer of 1948 Nationalist China was facing
military collapse. In view of the critical situation the students
decided to hold a prayer meeting for their country at 9 a.m.
daily in the guest hall. "Peter" also prepared a "manifesto"
setting forth clearly the position of the Peking Student Fellowship which he read to the group on July 7th. About this
time, too, the Fellowship bid a proud farewell to its first
missionary, a graduate doctor who was responding to a call
to go to the north-west of the country. There he joined the
staff of the Borden Memorial Hospital in Lanzhou, Gansu,
which was operated by the CIM and had originally been
founded to reach Tibetans and Muslims with the gospel.

As the time for our second summer conference approached, careful planning again preceded it. The site was
once more the old imperial stables-turned-orphanage behind
the Summer Palace. Everyone except the main guests slept
on the hard ground. Calvin Chao and Wang Mingdao were
the speakers, and the latter, who was celebrating his wedding
anniversary, testified to twenty years of married happiness
in the service of God. Each day began with physical training
exercises and group prayer meetings, while the preaching
and teaching of the speakers had the darkening future in
view. Swimming in the nearby Jade Fountain stream and

picnics to neighbouring beauty spots provided wonderfully happy fellowship. An impromptu choir rendered the Hallelujah Chorus quite professionally.

This second conference was marked by a deep spiritual hunger for the Word of God, the students having progressed from the immature and emotional stage of earlier days to greater maturity. Everyone sensed the urgency to know God more fully, and the prophetic words "From now on our work will be the work of prayer!" were often repeated. The young people well knew that under Communism the freedom to witness and evangelise which they had hitherto enjoyed would be severely curtailed if not entirely denied them and that prayer would be the only activity impossible to restrict. Time was already running out, but strong foundations had been laid for the future.

After that memorable conference autumn drew on, the leaves of the trees in the Western Hills turned to a glory of red and gold, and President Chiang Kai-shek paid a hurried visit to see the "fall" colours for the last time. Manchuria was already lost and refugee students from that area were pouring into Peking, some with tragic tales to tell. In an already overcrowded city the only places for them to lodge were in the various temple grounds. Yet another student demonstration turned into a riot; the police lost their nerve and opened fire, wounding some of the refugee students, and anger flared. I accompanied some Christian students on a visit to the wounded in hospital with words of comfort. As the refugee situation grew worse, members of the Student Fellowship held evangelistic meetings in the temples and open spaces where the refugees were camping out, inviting any who wished to join our meetings at No. 33. When the first snow of winter fell and the cold winds from the Gobi began to blow, the plight of the young people sleeping under the open sky beneath their thin coverlets was bitter indeed. We therefore advertised a soup kitchen at No. 33 which immediately became very popular with the hungry refugees.

The local military situation became increasingly critical

as the Communist armies massed for an assault on Peking itself. The US consul urgently advised all American citizens to leave, and a US naval vessel arrived in Tientsin to evacuate foreign nationals. On November 17th, after prayerful consideration, it seemed right to allow my wife and small daughter to leave. Chinese friends gave them an affectionate send-off at the station as I escorted them on a refugee "special" taking 200 foreigners to embark at Tientsin. After the ship had sailed early the next morning I returned to an empty house at No. 33, only to receive instructions a few days later to proceed to Shanghai. As I spoke to the Student Fellowship for the last time on November 28th, I was again deeply moved. I recalled what God had done in so many lives and could not help wondering what trials and suffering lay ahead of them.

Saying goodbye to Mr Wang Mingdao, with whom I had enjoyed much close fellowship and partnership in the student work, was not easy. His autobiography *These Fifty Years* had just been published, and he presented me with one of the first copies off the press. An antique fan which had belonged to his family for generations and which Mr Wang presented to us as a parting gift has been a constant reminder, if such were needed, to pray for the Lord's good and faithful servant during his twenty-two years of imprisonment. During that time he had no Bible but was daily sustained by the Scriptures which he had memorised and by favourite hymns which he sang to himself.

It is of interest to compare the end of the two Christian groups in Peking. The Student Christian Movement group, believing that under a Marxist government their ideal of a socialist utopia was about to dawn, voluntarily disbanded soon after the Communists took the city. The Peking Student Christian Fellowship, on the other hand, continued its witness to the Word of God and the power of the gospel for another six years, long after Peking had again become the capital city of China. The Fellowship was evicted from No. 33 but found alternative premises in the Union Church and did not disband until 1955 at the time of Wang Mingdao's arrest, against which they had made a strong protest. But what happened to these Christian students?

An American doctor, married to a Chinese lady, who stayed on in Peking wrote to me saying that as the Christians graduated and were posted all over China they were creating small oases of spiritual life amid the desert of Marxism. And what happened so wonderfully in Peking was being duplicated in almost every university in China. It is plain to see how the post-war student revival was a part of the divine preparation of a new generation of leaders whom the rapidly growing Church of the 1980s would so desperately need. Not only have the oases remained and multiplied, but now the desert rejoices and blossoms abundantly (Isaiah 35:1,2). Surely our God reigns in China. But what of individuals?

"Peter" himself had decided to go to Fuller Theological Seminary in the USA to prepare himself for future service in China. While he was a guest at our home we had tried to prepare him for life in the West, showing him, among other things, how to manipulate Western cutlery; but disposing of a poached egg with a knife and fork proved quite beyond his powers: it was swallowed whole in one mouthful!

Another very frequent guest, almost a member of the family, was a high school boy called "Henry" whose father was a doctor serving with the Communist army. Henry already spoke English well and wanted to improve, so he assisted me with my Chinese correspondence. Having very little money and being always hungry, he often joined us at our family table and even told goodnight stories to our children. Like Peter's, Henry's name was added to our prayer list, and for thirty years we faithfully remembered to pray for him once a week without anything to break the silence. Then, in 1979, he found out our address and a wonderful correspondence began. "What you did for us in Peking", he wrote "was exactly right for us young Chinese Christians at that time." He had gone on to study medicine in Tientsin and is now high up in the medical profession in China and engaged in cancer research at a provincial medi-

cal college. He has maintained a steady Christian witness
and, having survived twelve years of fearful persecution and
imprisonment, is today a leader among the numerous house
churches in his province. One of his letters reported a
reunion in Peking of some of the members of the Peking and
Tientsin Christian fellowships:

> While I was in Peking we had very good fellowship in the
> Lord. All of us were members of the Christian student
> body of Peking and Tientsin. Most of us have suffered
> during the past long difficult period, but now have been
> rehabilitated and are chief engineers or associate pro-
> fessors in universities. We prayed together and encour-
> aged one another in the Lord's Word.

Yet another medical student who had found Christ
through the Bible classes at the college is now the senior
doctor in a region where he also ministers to over 1,000
Christians. When we left that same region in 1940 there
were probably fewer than 200 believers.

The same American doctor who wrote about the oases
enclosed the following message printed on thin rice paper
and written by an unknown hand:

> True faith in God does not imply that we anticipate an
> easy future or believe that God will intervene to crown
> our righteous cause with an early victory. Faith is not
> confidence in God's willingness to serve those who seek
> His support. Faith is surrender to the will of God, even
> though that will may include the dark night of Geth-
> semane or the anguish of Calvary. Faith is serene trust in
> God's ability to use all human forces and passions for the
> fulfilment of His eternal purposes. It is a divinely inspired
> conviction that God's plans cannot be frustrated, that
> even the wrath of man can be made to praise Him.

The man of faith reads both his Bible and the book of
history. He beholds there the eternal unity of God's message and method. He sees clearly the guiding hand of God

in all the movements of the centuries and the changing fortunes of individuals and nations. Yes, "the Lord God Omnipotent reigneth". He is still Lord of His own creation.

There may have been many dark nights in the world's history, but the Sun of Righteousness has always risen to gild the eastern hills with the entrancing dawn of a new day of peace and progress. The God who is "the same yesterday and today and for ever" still controls His own universe. God's tomorrow will be brighter than today.

A prophetic voice, indeed, out of Communist China!

10 Favoured Province (1948–49)

> "The Lord reigns; let the earth rejoice; let the coastlands be glad!"
>
> *Psalm 97:1*

After leaving Peking, my wife went immediately to join her sister and brother-in-law who were working in the southern province of Zhejiang; and a week or two later I followed. The Nationalist armies were then in full retreat, and refugees were fleeing from the north in search of imaginary safety in the south.

As the train for Zhejiang pulled into the junction there was a mad scramble by hundreds of passengers waiting to get on board. On realising that entry through the doors would be impossible, I clambered through a window with my luggage along with others! Once inside the coach I found myself firmly wedged, with people sitting on the floor all down the aisles as well as on the seats and even occupying the toilets. Scores unable to get inside the coaches clambered on to the roof, where they patiently sat on their bedrolls – some even suspended themselves beneath the coaches! Among the passengers were men in uniform escorting their wives and families to safety, and, before long, arguments arose: "Why aren't you at the front fighting the Reds?" And arguments sometimes led to blows. It was a weary fifteen-hour journey, but Quxian was reached at last and a happy family Christmas was celebrated a week later.

Zhejiang ("forked stream") is a province of great beauty and variety: forest-clad mountains and hills, lovely rivers and streams, ancient bridges of architectural charm, bamboo groves, vineyards, world-famous tea plantations and walled cities of which Hangzhou, the capital, is the queen. This city, associated with Suzhou for beauty, lies on the shores of an enchanting lake rimmed with ancient and beautiful temples and pagodas. On the coast, Ningbo, where Hudson Taylor spent much of his first term in China, was one of the five original treaty ports opened to Western merchants and missionaries by the terms of the 1842 Treaty of Nanking.

Christian work began in Zhejiang soon after the year of that treaty, when the London Missionary Society opened a church and a school in Ningbo. The Church Missionary Society also had its representative; and Dr Parker, of the Chinese Evangelisation Society which was first represented by Hudson Taylor, had opened a hospital in that city. It was there that Hudson Taylor first met and married his wife Maria.

One of Hudson Taylor's early converts was Lae Djün, a carpenter who had gone on to become a mature Christian and a valuable fellow worker. He had travelled with Hudson Taylor to London to assist in the translation of the Ningbo New Testament, and his daughter subsequently married the great and influential Pastor T. K. Ren of Hangzhou, whose autobiography bore the title *The Tamarisk Garden Blessed by Rain*. It was this man who in 1928 presided at the wedding of Mr and Mrs Wang Mingdao, the bride being a native of that city.

After the founding of the China Inland Mission in Britain in 1865, Hudson Taylor returned to Zhejiang to set up his first mission station in Hangzhou where the Church Missionary Society and other societies were already well established. After the "Lammermuir Party", (so named after the vessel on which they, the first group of CIM missionaries, had sailed to China) had acquired enough language to understand and be understood, they dispersed to other cities in the province to evangelise and to plant churches. One man, Stott, whom Hudson Taylor had accepted despite his having a wooden leg, was placed in

Wenzhou, a beautifully situated city on the coast. So well
did he lay the foundations that the Wenzhou church became
the largest and the strongest ever to be planted by the China
Inland Mission; Hudson Taylor himself baptised the first
converts. Gradually other churches sprang up throughout
the province, and regular local Bible schools ensured a
church with strong roots. At a later stage a residential
Bible school in Hangzhou trained many future pastors. The
strength of the churches was severely tested in 1927 when,
at the outset of the civil war, the province was overrun by
Communist armies. Missionaries had to leave, and Christians were forced to endure violent campaigns launched
against them. When the missionaries returned a year later,
churches willingly accepted the policy of devolution of responsibilities from the former to themselves and the "three-
self" policy was gradually implemented.

During the 1930s Watchman Nee in Shanghai began
training leaders for the expansion of his assemblies, the
major expansion taking place in the coastal provinces of
Fujian and Zhejiang. In some cases churches which had
been founded by missionaries were taken over by Nee's
"Little Flock", as his assemblies were nicknamed; but in
many instances his evangelists established entirely new
churches. By 1940, in Zhejiang alone, they had listed 262
assemblies with a total membership of 39,000. Solid Bible
teaching by Chinese teachers not only ensured the survival
of the churches in the years of persecution to come, but also
laid the foundation for the spectacular numerical growth of
the churches in both coastal provinces from the late 1970s
onwards.

While we were staying in Quxian we discovered a school
which had been evacuated from the northern province of
Henan. As the boys and girls spoke a dialect that we understood, visits to the school, where Christians on the staff and
among the pupils held regular services, kept us busy. People
separated from home and family and fearful and uncertain
about the future were prepared to listen to the gospel.
Nationalist resistance to the Communist armies was crum-

bling rapidly, and clearly the time was short before Communism would conquer. These young people desperately needed a living faith which would endure under an oppressive regime. The Chinese New Year provided the usual excitement both for the Chinese and ourselves as the din of firecrackers rent the air and people paraded the streets in new clothes. The traditional strips of red paper bearing seasonal slogans were pasted afresh outside the doors of every home, while friends and relatives exchanged gifts and indulged in plenty of good food. But this was the last such carefree celebration! During the first month of the year all the churches held conferences which, at a time of great crisis, provided valuable opportunities to minister to Christians the comforting and strengthening Word of God.

After these meetings, at the invitation of the Wenzhou church, I set off on the six days' journey to minister to leaders of the country churches there. The limited bus service on the first three-day stage meant either no bus at all that day or standing for hours on end in a very crowded and jolting vehicle. But each night provided golden opportunities to share God's Word with fellow Christians, sixty in one town and 100 in another. On the final run in the dark to the bank of the River On, everyone was fearful of a possible bandit attack.

The second stage of the journey was by river boat, little bigger than a punt on the River Cam. It was already loaded with a cargo of bamboo leaves. The six passengers had just enough room to lie down on deck at night, a bamboo awning protecting them from sun and rain. The river flows down to the sea through magnificent scenery, its waters alternately shallow and deep, with calm stretches and lively rapids, the boatmen sailing, poling, paddling or towing the craft as appropriate. Each night we moored the boat, lit the lamps and shared a simple meal. By day we watched cormorants diving for fish, while other fishermen used explosives to stun the fish, which then floated to the surface. Fear of attack was never far from our minds, and those explosions kept us edgy! Two days and two nights brought us to Wenxi, where a motor launch took thirty or forty craft like our own in tow for the final six hours of the journey to Wenzhou.

Dr Shao, a church elder, was at the wharf to welcome me, and for the next five days there was scarcely a spare minute between the meetings. The city had two large and flourishing churches, and the Christian presence was there for all to see, many of the shops being owned by Christians – ten in one street alone – and all closed on Sundays. Wenzhou has a very distinct dialect of its own, and this fact has served to isolate the area and make the people very independent. My addresses had to be interpreted.

Four or five hundred elders representing the very numerous country churches had gathered for the meetings. Having come from the war zone, my burden was again the message of 1 Peter, and I told the story of the student work in Peking and described the attitude of the students to the future. But those good people could hardly believe that the Communists would ever reach their area or even succeed in crossing the Yangzi River, so I urged on them the necessity to gird themselves for the fiery trial which lay ahead. Who was then to know the intense suffering this church was to endure and the remarkable future that would follow when it would eventually experience such fantastic growth that in 1980 one in eight of the population would have become Christians? A sovereign God was even then, in 1949, preparing to manifest His glory to the world through this remarkable church.

The Christians showed me typical Chinese generosity and hospitality and after entertaining me to a feast in the best restaurant in town, the elders gave me a warm send-off as I boarded my Chinese "punt" ready to sail at dawn. I was the church's last foreign visitor before the city fell to the Communists later in the year, and those meetings were the last of their kind before the curtain fell. God had spoken, and hearts had been prepared.

The river journey in reverse allowed leisure to revel in the peace and beauty of God's creation though man's world was in turmoil. After changing from river boat to buses one bus broke down at a spot where two had been held up by bandits the previous day, and soldiers stood guard while repairs were carried out. Finally, thanks to a Christian station-master, a free ride on an open wagon of a goods train took me right back to Quxian. Soon, after seeing off three of our children on the journey back to school in Guling, the rest of the family left to return to Shanghai. On the way we stopped for two days in lovely Hangzhou to renew our friendship with Frank and Bessie England, Frank having been one of the five young men who made up the "vanguard" of the Two Hundred in 1929. He possessed an exceptional gift as a Bible teacher and was on the staff of the Bible institute. It is impossible to exaggerate the importance of the role of all such training grounds in almost every province in China. In schools like this one, God was preparing thousands of educated youth to become suffering servants in the years ahead. They would one day become the teachers and leaders of the churches in the "underground" period and later in the more open era that followed when household churches would multiply. The many pre-1949 Bible schools thus had a strategic role in God's plan for the future of His Church in China.

It was a privilege to have spent even a month or two in an area where God had already built a living church with living stones nurtured on the living Word (1 Peter 1–2); but no one could then have foreseen what far greater things God was yet to do in the years ahead in that favoured province.

11   Battle for Shanghai (1949–51)

"The blessed and only Sovereign, King of kings
and Lord of lords . . . to Him be honour and eternal
dominion. Amen!"

1 Timothy 6:15, 16

Shanghai, China's fantastic metropolis, built largely with
foreign money and skills on the mud flats beside the
Huangpu River, has throughout its history been a cosmopolitan trading post between East and West. After being
designated a treaty port it developed rapidly. The original
Chinese city was left untouched, but "foreign" settlements
grew up nearby: first the British Concession, then the
French, and finally an area administered by Americans. The
construction of multi-storeyed banks, hotels, hospitals, residential flats and office buildings had involved driving piles
deep into the swamp for foundations. The area is still so
low-lying that even now the city is frequently flooded when
winds and tides combine to cause this periodic inconvenience.

In its heyday Shanghai had flourished, and Western
merchants and their Chinese compradores or agents had
grown very rich on the China trade. The city had provided
every kind of diversion for foreigners: a racecourse, sports
grounds, a golf course, theatres, cinemas, restaurants, clubs
of every sort – and the "world's longest bar"! Foreign
shipping companies had operated services up the Yangzi
and along the coast. The Hong Kong and Shanghai Bank
building had once dominated the Bund or waterfront of the
Huangpu. Merchant vessels of all nations had carried their

cargoes to and from this great port. Here the P & O passenger liners from England had reached their final destination. Foreign warships lay at anchor in the river as well as up river, an unwelcome reminder of the Western imperialism which had dominated China for so many years. From the beginning, Christian missions had set up their headquarters in this strategic city.

Ten miles outside Shanghai itself, on the railway line from Shanghai to Woosung, lies the village of Jiangwan where Miss Ruth Brittain, an American who had once taught at the Ginling Theological Seminary in Nanjing, founded the China Bible Seminary for women. The seminary attracted students immediately, and its future was looking bright when in 1927, during the first Communist uprising, its buildings were burnt to the ground. In faith they were rebuilt, though their first occupants were the Chinese soldiers who had fortified them against the Japanese invaders; many friends had feared for the safety of the seminary. Since the area continued to be unsafe Miss Brittain rented premises in the British settlement and in about 1937 reopened the seminary with fifty-six students, this time including several young men. Then, as war broke out four years later, all foreigners were interned by the Japanese and the seminary again had to close its doors.

As soon as the war ended in 1945 no time was lost before reopening the seminary on its old site in Jiangwan. The buildings were renovated and new residences were erected for both men and women. It was in 1949 that Miss Brittain, whose fellow worker was Miss Audrey Johnson of the China Inland Mission, invited us to join the staff. Pastor David Yang, our old friend and colleague, was already a much-loved teacher there and it was a joy to share in the training of many splendid men and women. The discipline was strict, high academic standards were demanded, and a fine spiritual tone was maintained. The China Bible Seminary was yet another "barracks" where Christian recruits were being trained and hardened in readiness for the long and fierce campaigns ahead. They were being equipped for spiritual warfare and prepared to endure hardness as good soldiers of Jesus Christ. We were soon at home both in our teaching and in our personal relationships with the students, who came freely to our flat for meals and to share their problems. We joined in the prayer meetings and fellowship meetings where prayer was offered for the many graduates serving God in China and throughout Asia: over 200 in China proper; twenty-five in Manchuria; six in Xinjiang (Turkestan) including two with the Back to Jerusalem Band; three in Xizang and Tibet; two in Burma; eight in Thailand; fifteen in Malaya; ten in the Philippines; three in Borneo; eight in Java; and two in northern Australia.

In Shanghai work among university students was at fever pitch, and David Adeney, the student adviser, was a frequent and welcome visitor to our flat to discuss plans for the future and to pray over the many problems. By mid-March 1949 most of north China was in Communist hands, and the Red armies massed north of the River Yangzi were demanding the unconditional surrender of the Nationalist armies. In early April, Christian students attending a conference at the Baptist seminary were deeply conscious of God's presence in their midst when suddenly, on April 7th, a news flash reported that Communist units had succeeded in crossing the Yangzi near Nanjing. Although the students had realised that sooner or later this event was inevitable, the actual news came as a shock and they seemed dazed.

In the middle of the conference I was hastily recalled to Jiangwan because Nationalist soldiers were camping in the grounds, using the chapel as a rest centre and mounting guns all around the seminary. Nanjing fell on April 23rd, and two days later President Chiang Kai-shek and his government boarded a cruiser and sailed away to Taiwan, taking with them all the gold in the Bank of China. The following day, US warships moved down river to the Lower Yangzi; British warships up river were fired on, and HMS *Amethyst* made her gallant dash for the coast under heavy fire. After Suzhou had fallen on April 27th, Shanghai, the greatest prize of all, lay within the grasp of the Communist armies. Street defences were erected by the defenders, all universities were closed and some students were arrested. The Jiangwan railway station now became a scene of feverish activity as tanks and armoured cars were unloaded for the defence of Shanghai. By May 5th Peking had fallen and Hangzhou had been abandoned.

Now the crucial battle for Shanghai was near. In view of the serious situation the principal of the seminary gave permission to overseas students to leave if they chose to do so. On May 8th a Chinese colonel requisitioned the men's residence for his regimental headquarters and ordered the digging of trenches in the garden. On the 13th, gunfire in the direction of Woosung shook our buildings. From then on, night after night, sleep became difficult as a non-stop artillery duel rumbled and roared. On the 16th, the colonel called me in to say that his regiment was about to pull out and evacuate to Taiwan. It was therefore clear that the Nationalists were now preparing nothing more than a rear-guard action in defence of Shanghai. "Don't trust the Communists!" warned the colonel. "They will at first be all fair words, but you will discover their real intentions later on!" I thanked him for his advice. That night, after the withdrawal of his troops, the ammunition dump in the nearby athletic stadium was detonated and the explosion shook buildings violently for miles around. Unable to sleep and half-deafened by the din of battle, we watched the skies light up with gun flashes and explosions. On the 18th, as trainloads of demoralised Nationalist soldiers rumbled through the station, the Communists stormed the Woosung and Pootung forts in an attempt to cut off the Nationalist retreat. Resistance in Shanghai itself ceased on May 25th and the city surrendered, but our turn was yet to come.

At 7 a.m. on the 26th a loud burst of small-arms fire suddenly erupted all around us. We all lay flat on the floor and waited for the firing to cease. With the Communists meeting no opposition, we too were soon "liberated". Communist army officers paid us courtesy visits and groups of their soldiers straggled into the seminary grounds to dry their uniforms or cook themselves a hot meal. Despite the surrounding turmoil and general uncertainty, the seminary routine continued uninterrupted!

One day as we were entertaining visitors to lunch, we watched with amazement a column of Nationalist prisoners marching past the front entrance of the seminary towards an assembly point at the railway station. Suddenly, some of them broke ranks and darted into the seminary grounds to the nearest building, which happened to be the women's residence. There they hastily ripped off their tell-tale uniforms and escaped in their underwear over a fence and in the direction of Shanghai. I did all I could to speed their departure and to distribute the abandoned clothing to grateful neighbours. We feared possible repercussions from the Communist authorities, but there were none.

Remarkably soon telephone and postal services were restored, and life, both in Shanghai and Jiangwan, returned to a new kind of normal. Never before had the famed Communist guerilla armies, familiar with governing rural communities, faced the task of administering a modern city of six million people; but by taking over the entire civil service the transition was effected with scarcely a hitch. Naturally we wondered what the future held for the seminary, but for the time being we carried on as usual.

June was hot and humid, and classes were moved to early morning so as to avoid the worst of the heat, while bullfrogs in the neighbouring swamp kept up their monotonous chorus. Nationalist planes began occasional hit-and-run bombing raids on key installations in Shanghai. On July 7th a huge, noisy victory parade wended its way through the streets of the city with a sea of red banners waving and drums pulsating. As the season of violent storms and floods approached, we realised that the seminary was probably in its last days. The Huangpu dykes threatened to overflow, and on July 25th gale-force winds blew out many of the seminary windows and the chapel roof collapsed. For twenty-four hours the typhoon blew, and when it did finally cease classes had to be suspended so that everyone could join in clearing up the debris, repairing the damage and restoring the boundary fences. As term ended so did our work in the seminary, which first tried to avoid closure by amalgamating with an orphanage but was finally handed over to the new Communist authorities. As we parted from the students and moved back into Shanghai, we wondered what purposes God had for these dedicated young people. In retrospect it is clear that they and thousands of other Bible school graduates were being prepared by Him to fulfil His purposes in the 1980s when millions of new converts would so desperately need trained teachers and leaders.

The former Nationalist government was now a government in exile in Taiwan. While Nationalist planes embarked on nuisance raids on the Mainland, the People's Liberation Army completed its conquest of China, region by region. Everywhere the PLA went hoardings promised freedom of religious belief, as in the Russian Constitution which became the model for the first of several successive Chinese Constitutions. And many Christians felt less fearful and somewhat reassured, especially when the new government began to achieve spectacular results. With the introduction of a "People's Currency" the new authorities miraculously halted a long-standing and runaway inflation in its tracks. On October 1st, Chairman Mao Zedong proclaimed from Peking's Gate of Heavenly Peace the foundation of the People's Republic of China. Ten days of excited celebrations followed.

The question of how long missionaries could continue their work in China under a Communist regime was uppermost in everyone's mind: there were both pessimists and optimists. Workers in inland provinces began to feel the pressures from often very young and inexperienced cadres operating by the book. In Shanghai, we held meetings to study Marxist theory and practice while continuing our work with heightened urgency. Clearly time was running out, and so much was waiting to be done. In seeking to prepare the Chinese Church for the future the China Inland

Mission judged Christian literature to be a high priority. The Christian Literature Society had in its prime published some useful books, but in recent years most of its authors had been of a liberal and left-wing persuasion. The Religious Tract Society had served evangelical missions and churches well but not well enough, and the number of good evangelical publications was pathetically small. There were, however, sufficient to enable the China Inland Mission to provide every pastor in China, as far as possible, with a small "library" of a score of useful books. The CIM did not go into the publishing business seriously until after leaving China, but since then book publishing has been a major concern of the Overseas Missionary Fellowship in Hong Kong, Manila, Djakarta, Taipei and Bangkok.

The first book for which the CIM was responsible was the biography of Hudson Taylor, the translator of which was a local Christian Chinese doctor. It fell to me to edit the translation carefully, both as to the content and the accuracy. The result was a volume which immediately became a best-seller and has been singled out as one of the most helpful books circulating in China today. Seeing this book through the process of translation, printing and distribution took many months.

Another work selected for translation was Halley's *Bible Commentary*, and for a year or two "Stephen", a former Peking student friend, and I worked closely together in this task, though time did not permit its completion before we had to leave China. Stephen's wife (we attended their wedding), yet another of our student friends in Peking, also assisted me in the production of a new hymnbook. *Hymns of Universal Praise* had been widely used by the denominational churches, and CIM churches had their long-established *Hymns of Praise*; but the time had now come for a more up-to-date and lively collection in which modern terminology and literary form would be taken into account and antiquated translations by early missionaries replaced. This hymn-book, with an introduction written by David Yang, proved a welcome addition to the worship of the churches.

Literary tasks like these kept me at full stretch right up to the time of departure from Shanghai, while weekly Old Testament lectures at the Baptist seminary continued until the very last moment. Autumn brought cold and snow, but a surprise visit from a group of former fellow workers in Hebei, all known personally to us both, was a welcome tonic for everyone at headquarters. These men and women had been without missionary fellowship since 1939 and had suffered for Christ's sake, first under the Japanese and then under Communist rule; but all testified warmly to God's faithfulness. They had come to Shanghai specially to express their deep gratitude to the CIM for its many years of service to China. I was able to show them around the city, and we visited the various Christian bookshops and the offices of the Bible Society. These were tried and hardened warriors, and they encouraged us all in a conviction that we were leaving behind in China a living Church built of living stones.

There were other visitors as well. Because of my father-in-law's close friendship with Watchman Nee, I too enjoyed his friendship and frequently profited from his ministry and hospitality. There had sometimes been mutual criticism between the Little Flock and the CIM, and so we invited Watchman Nee and five of his co-workers to coffee in our flat. There the staff of CIM headquarters spent several hours with them in discussion and prayer.

"What about the future?" we asked. "What can we do to help the Church in China while we are away?"

"What we need very badly is more good commentaries," was the reply. "So please work on the translation of commentaries like those by Bishop Lightfoot!"

"And when we return to China," we asked, "what will you require of us?"

"Next time you come, come not as missionaries," was the reply, "but as teaching elders in our churches."

Then followed a question which expressed the deep anxieties of our guests: "How long is this suffering going to continue?"

To which our reply had to be: "We fear that the suffering has only just begun and that the Chinese Church must brace itself for much greater suffering in the future."

Surely enough, Watchman Nee was to spend fifteen years in prison before his death in 1972, and many members of his assemblies were to suffer too. But thirty years on the Little Flock assemblies would also be sharing in the growth of the house churches and in the nurture of new believers all over China. It was a solemn moment as we all knelt and committed one another into the hands of the One who had promised to be with His people to the very end.

The political battle for Shanghai might be over, but the spiritual battle for the soul of China was only just beginning; and that would be a battle that would leave many Christians wounded and scarred:

> Captain Beloved, battle wounds were Thine,
> May I not wonder if some hurt be mine.
> Rather, O Lord, let my deep wonder be
> That I may share a battle wound with Thee!
>   Swords drawn, swords drawn
>   Up to the gate of Heaven
>   For us swords drawn
>   Up to the gate of Heaven!

Amy Carmichael

12   Shackled (1949–58)

"Your divine throne endures for ever and ever.
Your royal sceptre is a sceptre of equity."

Psalm 45:6

"The balloon has gone up!" was the immediate comment
of the CIM director when late one night I reported to him
on the meeting which had just been held in the Shanghai
YMCA. The year was 1950, and Christian representatives
of the Shanghai community had been listening to an account
of an unprecedented and epoch-making meeting in Peking
between the prime minister Zhou Enlai and selected members of the National Christian Council. At that meeting
the terms of the "Christian Manifesto" were agreed. They
plainly committed the Church to dissociate itself from all
"imperialist" associations and to submit itself to the direction of the Communist Party. Never before had any Chinese
government given such high-level attention to the Christian
Church, and the delegates accepted this as an honour. But
that meeting signalled the end of an era: the Manifesto left
no doubt that missionaries must soon withdraw from China.
Those Christian leaders had signed the death warrant of the
foreign missionary movement in China.

As far as Protestants were concerned, that movement had
begun with the 1842 Treaty of Nanking. Robert Morrison,
living in the Portuguese colony of Macao, had already
translated the Bible into literary Chinese but had never been
permitted to reside on Chinese soil. The treaty which concluded the first Opium War had secured the cession of the

island of Hong Kong to the British and the opening of five
treaty ports – Canton, Amoy, Fuzhou, Ningbo and Shanghai
– to foreign trade and residence. Missionaries, who up to
that time had been excluded from China and who had been
waiting in Malaya and Java for the door into that country to
open, quickly made their way first to Shanghai and then
to the other ports to start Christian work.

Seen through the eyes of the Chinese, the Treaty of
Nanking and that of Tientsin eight years later were totally
unjust and unequal, and acts of blatant imperialism. Since
missionaries were among the first people to take advantage
of the treaty terms, they have always been regarded as the
cultural spearhead of imperialism. That great and proud
nation has felt a deep sense of shame at its treatment by the
British and other Western powers; it has never forgiven
Britain for the crime of the "unequal treaties" which
allowed the exploitation of China's resources and forced
its people to accept opium grown in India in exchange for
such commodities as tea and silk. The Boxer Uprising of
1900 was to be the culmination of sixty years of antagonism
and resentment towards all foreigners. Dr Sun Yat-sen,
the Christian founder of the first Chinese republic, con-
demned the treaties in his classic *Three People's Principles*
which were taught to China's youth for a whole generation
after the 1911 Nationalist revolution, thereby further stoking
the fires of hatred for all foreigners. The Chinese people
were also made to believe that missionaries were paid agents
of their governments; and no denial of the charge was ever
accepted. The Communists forcefully pursued the theme of
foreign imperialism in the 1920s and used it to vilify the
Christian Church. Yet the facts are that missionaries had
always been unanimous in condemning the opium traffic
and that it was Christians in the British Parliament who
fought successfully to have it ended. The entry of missionaries into China in the wake of the gunboats had certainly
been an unfortunate historical coincidence, but Christian
missions have never consciously been part of any imperialist
or colonialist activity directed against China.

If history had militated against missions in China, so also did Marxist theory. Religion, according to Karl Marx, is an unscientific and harmful superstition, an opiate to lull the poor into indifference to their lot and so prevent social change. Thus Marxists have presented Christianity to the Chinese as an evil thing, both because it allied itself with the imperialist powers to achieve the political subjugation of China and because, according to Marx, it is a false superstition and an instrument of oppression. Marxist dogma and an accident of history have therefore combined to present Christianity in the blackest of guises. Furthermore, a nation proud of its sophisticated native philosophers has always despised and feared Christianity as an extraneous foreign cult which threatened to undermine the very fabric of its society. This last fact and the issue of ancestral worship were, according to Professor Lin Yutang, the main reasons why Christianity had made such slow progress in China.

When the Communists seized power in 1949 there were fewer than one million Protestant believers in China, and that after a century of great missionary activity, a vast expenditure of money and the sacrifice of many lives. It required the departure of the missionaries in 1951 and thirty years of freedom from missionary association to alter the "foreign" image of the Christian religion and to give the Church today some degree of respectability in the eyes of the Chinese people.

The "Christian Manifesto" was originally drawn up by premier Zhou Enlai and then, with minor emendations, accepted by the deputation of church leaders. It duly received nationwide publicity through the press, and Christians were invited to sign their names to it as evidence of their approval. The number said to have signed the Manifesto was 40,000, and in so doing they assented to the charge of being agents of foreign imperialism and promised to sever all links with imperialism and colonialism. They likewise pledged their loyalty to the Communist Party and promised total subservience to a Marxist state.

The first consequence of the publication of the Manifesto

was the early withdrawal from China of all foreign missionaries. Clearly in the new political climate their continued
presence, however welcome it had been in the past, could
now only embarrass Chinese Christians and threaten the
Church's very survival. So in 1951–2 a general exodus took
place.' Members of the China Inland Mission held on for
as long as possible, but in remote parts of the country
their position became increasingly intolerable as Communist
armies completed the conquest. In January 1951, therefore,
the critical decision to withdraw was taken. Then, in a
well-planned operation, groups of missionaries and their
families began leaving for Hong Kong at regular intervals.
We ourselves said goodbye to all our friends, some of whom
bravely came to the railway station to see us off; others met
us in Canton to help us change trains. And so in May we
joined our three older children, who had left ahead of us, in
crowded Hong Kong. Camp life in army huts gave time to
reflect sadly on the past and to contemplate the future; a
future which, for our family, was to be in England.

"The Manifesto", wrote *Heavenly Wind* (*Tien Feng*), the
official Christian magazine, "will have historic significance
for Christianity in China." It did indeed mark the end of
over 140 years of Protestant missionary work – but how
fared the Church which the missionaries left behind?

The government department set up to deal with religion
was the Religious Affairs Bureau (RAB). This organisation
in turn created separate bodies to administer each religion:
for Roman Catholics the Catholic Patriotic Association,
which required the Chinese members of that faith to reject
Vatican control over their affairs; and for Protestants the
Three-Self Patriotic Movement, which was set up to direct
the affairs of that Church and which also required a complete
severance from all "imperialist" support and control. The
first chairman of the TSPM was Mr Y. T. Wu, a YMCA
secretary.

In April 1951, 158 selected church leaders were called to
Peking for an inaugural conference whose purpose was to
launch the TSPM, originally called the Three-Self Reform

Church. Only those leaders with "political awareness" had been invited to serve on the preparatory committees set up in 1950. The "three-self" slogan adopted in the 1920s by missionaries and the national church as a guide to the indigenisation of the Church was now given an entirely new twist by making it mean the total severance of the relationship between the Church in China and the Church universal; the slogan was thus given a political connotation totally absent from the original concept. It remains to this day a basic policy. C. M. Chen, a defector to the West who was for ten years an official of the RAB, once said that the dispute between Christians and Communists was not political but philosophical and that therefore the struggle against Christianity takes on the character of "an invisible battle". Thus the purpose of the government was not outright extermination but restriction, reformation and control. The Three-Self Patriotic Movement, Chen said, had been created with this end in view, and the government went to great lengths and expense in the early years of its rule to indoctrinate church leaders so as to make religion serve politics and render the Church politically harmless. Nothing secret could be allowed, and detailed files were kept on all church leaders and their activities.

A drastic purge of the Church immediately followed the publication of the Manifesto, coinciding with a wave of arrests and summary trials which held the whole country in the grip of fear. An "accusation" campaign singled out all pastors and leaders who had enjoyed special relations with missionaries and then, under the chairmanship of a government cadre, caused them to be pilloried by their own congregations and even by their closest colleagues. They were accused of being "pro-imperialist and pro-American reactionaries" or "corrupt elements". The prototype "accusation meeting" was held in Peking during the 1951 TSPM conference, when, in support of the process, its leaders quoted Jesus' condemnation of the Pharisees and its chairman Y. T. Wu compared it to the cleansing of the Temple. This tragic farce was a searing experience; and the humiliation, the loss of face, the fear drove some to suicide. Every church which in this way recognised its past sins of imperialist contamination and "repented" was then deemed to have passed through a process of "new birth" and so become eligible for government recognition. (Even Communists use the vocabulary of evangelism!) On January 10th the TSPM staged a huge, carefully rehearsed accusation meeting in the Shanghai Canidrome stadium where prominent local Christians were required to make their public confession. The meeting was obviously designed to humiliate and inflict a severe loss of face on America, on the missionary movement as a whole and on the Chinese Church itself.

Other results followed the accusation campaign: the TSPM forbade anyone "parasitically" to accept a salary from his congregation, and ministers were compelled to engage in productive labour on farms or in factories. Indoctrination in Marxism-Leninism-Mao Thought had already become a part of everyday life for the masses, but pastors and church workers were required to attend special extended courses for intensive indoctrination – a gruelling experience which left churches in no doubt about government policies and priorities. Churches had to obey Party direction, and loyalty to the State had to come before that to the Church. The outbreak of the war in Korea underlined the importance of patriotism, and a new slogan "Love country, love Church!" (and in that order) was given nationwide publicity. For many Christians this was reminiscent of the dilemma of the early Church "Christ or Caesar?", and since the slogan conflicted with their understanding of the Lordship of Christ they could not accept its implications.

In order further to denigrate foreign missionaries TSPM conferences were held in 1952 and 1954, both of which were financed by the government and took place under the chairmanship of its officials. Mr Wu's 1954 speech betrayed a mind obsessed with the delusion that the entire missionary movement in China had from the beginning been one of imperialist aggression and that Chinese Christianity had consistently been its tool: there was venom in every word.

Gutzlaff, Timothy Richard, Hudson Taylor and others were singled out by name and accused of misinterpreting the Scriptures, perverting Christian doctrine and creating divisions within the Church, thereby causing Chinese Christians to breathe the poison of imperialist thought. At a later date, the theological seminary in Nanjing was to collect "documentary evidence of missionary involvement in imperialist aggression", now on public display in its library. In 1982 a book entitled *Missions and Modern China* was published presenting a very warped and unhistorical version of missionary history.

The issue of whether the TSPM is, as it claims to be, a spontaneous, free and independent body of the Chinese Church or an organisation created by the Communist Party to carry out Party policy is hotly debated. The late Mr Wu, who before becoming the TSPM's first chairman was a senior official of the YMCA, a body well known for its liberal stance, had during the war with Japan become pro-Communist and an ardent student of Marxism. Writing in *Heavenly Wind* in 1958, he declared: "Without the Communist Party there would not have been the TSPM or the Christian Church . . . I love the Communist Party." In these words he plainly admitted that the TSPM had been the creation of the Communists.

On March 31st 1982 the Party's Central Committee issued a highly significant circular bearing the title *Concerning Our Country's Basic Standpoint and Policy on Religious Questions During the Socialist Period*. This document, published in *Red Flag*, is the most important statement on religious policy published since 1949, and I shall refer to it again. After claiming for the Chinese Government the credit for the early elimination of imperialist influences in the churches, for forwarding the "correct policy" of the "three selfs" and for changing Catholicism and Protestantism into "an independent religious undertaking of Chinese Christians", it defends what that government means by religious freedom and emphasises the limits to be imposed on such freedom. Then follow the key sentences: "All the patriotic religious organisations should obey the leadership of the Party and the government"; "Our Party committees at all levels must powerfully *direct* and *organise* all relevant departments, including the United Front departments, the Religious Affairs Bureau, etc."; "We must strengthen the organs of government *controlling religious affairs*." From this document it is plain that the TSPM has never been a free and spontaneous expression of the Church's life and is solely an instrument of Party policy. Devout Christians had failed to discern in Mr Wu the authentic marks of the true Christian, namely a devotion to the Word of God and a prayerful reliance on the Holy Spirit. They could not therefore conscientiously give their allegiance either to him or to an organisation so totally controlled by an atheist government. This attitude was to plunge hundreds of faithful Christians into long years of suffering.

Mr Wu commonly used to refer scathingly to evangelical Christians (by far the majority in China) as the "spiritual party", and this was by no means a compliment. His own liberal theology and the Biblical theology of evangelicals were poles apart, and the TSPM leaders saw clearly that the strongest opposition to State religious policies would come from evangelical Christians. It was equally clear to them and the government that two men stood out among evangelicals as the principal figures in opposition: Nee Do-sheng (Watchman Nee) of Shanghai and Wang Mingdao of Peking, both of whom had a very wide following, locally in their own churches and elsewhere as a result of their popular publications. During the "Five Antis" campaign of 1952 (anti-bribery, -tax evasion, -fraud, -theft of government property and -theft of state economic secrets), Nee was arrested on a charge of being a capitalist (he operated a factory to support Christians) and a landowner (he owned land and property in Fuzhou for the training of his workers), and held in custody pending a formal trial; four years later he was formally sentenced to fifteen years' imprisonment. A simultaneous violent campaign "to root out counter-revolutionaries" within the Watchman Nee assemblies com-

pelled the Little Flock churches in Shanghai to toe the
Three-Self line. After Nee had served his full sentence he
was released, but he died soon afterwards, in 1972.

Wang Mingdao of Peking, the other alleged opponent of
government religious policy, had already during the Sino-
Japanese War resisted attempts by the Japanese authorities
to make him take his church into a union of churches, so he
was no stranger to official opposition. Moreover, he had
always been totally uncompromising where Biblical truth
was concerned and an outspoken critic of China's liberal
theologians, the same men who were now heading the
TSPM. They had always deeply resented this and had
repeatedly tried to silence this powerful voice for freedom.
Up to 1955 Mr Wang continued to preach courageously in
China's new capital city and to publish his influential *Spiritual Food Quarterly*; but in 1954 the TSPM brought him before
a public accusation meeting at which a few voices actually
demanded the death penalty. However, the almost total
lack of support for any sanctions whatsoever compelled the
government to release him for the time being. It was then
that the Peking Student Christian Fellowship started their
"Oppose the persecution of Wang Mingdao!" campaign,
which received wide support even in China's new capital as
well as throughout the country. Mr Wang then continued
preaching to larger crowds than ever, and the winter evangelistic meetings of January 1955 were probably the most
fruitful he had ever conducted. In July, record attendances
filled the Tabernacle for two weeks of meetings at which Mr
Wang did not shrink from criticism of the TSPM and the
compromising evangelicals, such as Marcus Cheng, who
had thrown in their lot with the Communist Party.

In two pamphlets entitled *Truth or Poison?* and *Loyalty to
God Without Respect of Persons*, Mr Wang threw down the
gauntlet to the Three-Self leaders. They accepted the challenge, for opposition to their policies could no longer be
tolerated. During the 1955 TSPM conference in Peking six
prominent leaders of that organisation asked for a meeting
with Mr Wang, and were furious when this was refused.

Immediately the necessary machinery to silence the Lord's servant was set in motion. Mr Wang had already shared with Hu Feng, a Communist writer who had fallen from grace, a nationwide campaign to discredit them both; the press, secular and religious alike, had vilified him and listed his "crimes", though all the world knew that in his life, both private and public, it would be difficult to find fault with him for he practised what he preached: upright, disciplined living. On August 7th, Wang Mingdao delivered his last sermon to a tense and fearful congregation and distributed his final apologia "We because of our faith . . ." his own personal manifesto. That night the security police went to his home and arrested him; eighteen leading members of his congregation were arrested at the same time. Like Watchman Nee, Mr Wang received a fifteen-year sentence, but his was later increased to life imprisonment. Little was heard of him or his wife (in a separate prison) for over twenty years until their release in 1980 and 1979 respectively.

At the second national conference of the TSPM in 1960 Dr Wu Yifang, a vice-chairman, reported that "with the break-up of the counter-revolutionary ring headed by Wang Mingdao and Watchman Nee, most reactionary forces have been cleared out of the Church".

The Revd Marcus Cheng, a prominent evangelical leader and Bible seminary principal both before and during the war with Japan, and not unknown in the West, had at first welcomed what he had considered to be a genuine reform movement; he had even joined the Communist Party! But now, after years of trying to believe in the new order and of serving as a religious delegate in the People's Political Consultative Council (a kind of Lower House), he made an extraordinary outburst before that assembly in a speech in which he complained bitterly about infringement of religious freedom, the hostile attitude of certain cadres towards local rural churches and the uneven application of official policy. He boldly defended Christian belief and demanded respect for it, vigorously protesting against the blasphemy of many Party members and the abuse directed at religious believers even by high officials. The Council was stunned by this eloquent and fiery protest from a Party member who in the TSPM was second only to Y. T. Wu. The speech gained nationwide publicity through the *People's Daily* and *Heavenly Wind*, both of which, surprisingly, printed it in full. Marcus Cheng had gone as far as any Christian could go in his support of the new China and the TSPM; now his disillusionment was complete. So by 1958, the year in which the TSPM announced the unification of the Church, the churches were firmly under State control.

But even while, between 1951 and 1958, the TSPM was tightening its grip, evangelical Christians in many parts of China were refusing to accept the threatened stranglehold on their activities. Indigenous missionary societies like the Back to Jerusalem Band, the Central Asia Spiritual Work Team and the Christian Workers' Mission continued to recruit new members for their work of evangelism in Inner Mongolia, in Turkestan (Xinjiang) and on the Tibetan border. In Tihwa (Urumqi), the Xinjiang capital, nineteen converts were baptised. Elsewhere in the province, new churches were being established and existing churches experiencing revival. Among the Chinese missionaries there were several China Bible Seminary graduates. In the monastery town of Labrang in east Tibet, where the present Dalai Lama as a boy met missionaries who had given him Bibles, a number of Tibetans were baptised and others were turning to Christ. Reports from Yunnan in the south-west told of large church attendances among the tribespeople. After the departure of the missionaries from Anhui, church membership there had increased dramatically, including an addition of nearly 2,000 in one church alone; while in the coastal province of Zhejiang the already large Christian community was continuing to grow.

Peking and Shanghai were from the start the focal points of the Revolution; but in Shanghai, where Christians had already experienced their "baptism of fire", one church which had initiated an unbroken chain of prayer not surprisingly baptised 114 persons in 1953. In 1954, 900 university students held a four-day Christian conference in Shanghai. At the same time, eighty graduates decided to meet daily in the early mornings for Bible study and prayer while waiting to be posted to remote inland areas where, no doubt, they continue to maintain their witness. The Bible Society was still able to supply Scriptures and, as capital became available, even to print fresh editions to meet the continuing demand. All this, five years after the Revolution! In 1957 Christian students continued to meet for prayer and Bible study in nine of China's universities, and that same year they held yet another delegate conference in Swatow. Events like these were surprising in view of the fact that the young were everywhere being subjected to intensive Marxist re-education. Then, in 1958, the year of the Great Leap Forward, all parts of China reported numerous baptisms. In Henan, there was a phenomenal increase in church membership, thus anticipating the remarkable church growth in this province twenty-five years on. Even in the fateful year of 1961, at the height of the anti-rightist campaign and in Chairman Mao's own native province of Hunan, 170 individuals were baptised.

Clearly, many Christians were determined to "redeem the time", though the days were certainly evil. The Church was revealing an inner strength and resilience in the face of growing threats to its freedom and the mind-bludgeoning indoctrination or "brainwashing" which it shared with the whole nation. In the course of these almost daily study sessions, Christians inevitably became marked people: the Constitution might guarantee "freedom of religious belief", but it also allowed freedom "to oppose religious belief and to propagate atheism". Consequently all religion was interminably denounced as superfluous superstition, with Christians being given no liberty to reply. The author of the second psalm calls the vapourings of atheists laughable in the eyes of God, and records God's statement about His son: "I have set my King on Zion, my holy hill." Chinese Christians were clinging to the belief that God reigns supreme above every earthly power, and rejoicing in the certainty that one day every proud knee will bow to Jesus and every tongue that now denies Him will confess that He is Lord to the glory of God the Father.

13   Furnace of Affliction (1958–76)

"God reigns over the nations; God sits on His holy throne."

Psalm 47:8

During the first decade of the People's Government in China it was possible to follow the course of events there through what was written in the secular and religious press. Some international correspondents based in Peking were clearly sympathetic with the ideology of the new regime, and reported with enthusiasm the progress being made. Writers like Edgar Snow, Felix Green and Han Suyin wrote persuasively about the wonderful new China. Even China experts like Dr Joseph Needham of Cambridge University, whom we had entertained in Anshun during the war and who paid periodic visits to China, were uncritical in their praise. A Society of Friends mission to China brought back a glowing report of conditions in the People's Republic. But through various other channels much information did reach the outside world and it was possible to piece together a fairly accurate picture of what was going on. As for myself, I contributed a regular monthly feature called "Window on China" to the *East Asia Millions*; I also reported to periodical gatherings of China's friends meeting at the Church House, Westminster. In 1960 I published *Come Wind, Come Weather*, the story of the experiences of the Church from the time of the "liberation" in 1949 to 1959, including the Great Leap Forward. But by that time things had begun to go wrong for China and her leaders.

It was in May 1957 that Chairman Mao committed the first of what now, in 1984, most Chinese recognise as three major blunders which seriously mar his image as the "Great Helmsman". Each of these blunders exceeded its predecessor in gravity, and each brought the Christian Church into ever-increasing suffering. One writer has said that "the greatest feat of the present regime is that it has had the courage to denounce the disaster, fix blame and reverse course".

From Chairman Mao's point of view, the first seven years of his peasant revolution had gone very well. The early fifties had been a time of optimism when inflation, which had soared under the Nationalists, was quickly halted, the land reform programme (though it had cost three million lives) was completed and the peasants, who make up 80% of China's population, were freed from the tyranny of rapacious landlords. The country had proved her military strength by fighting the USA to a standstill in Korea; scientific farming and huge irrigation projects were increasing agricultural production; while enormous undertakings such as the San Men Dam on the Yellow River and the first of three bridges over the Yangzi at Nanjing had provided evidence of her people's immense engineering skills. Factories were producing everything from automobiles to aeroplanes, and communications were improving rapidly as rail and road mileage was greatly extended. Literacy was making great strides, and the medical services, with the aid of the part-time "barefoot doctors", were catering as never before for the whole population. The cleaning up of vice and the promotion of the ethic of unselfish service to the community seemed to suggest that a moral transformation was taking place among the Chinese. The colour magazines published in China and circulated world-wide portrayed a people relaxed, happy and free under a beneficent ruler who seemed to be the object of universal admiration – even affection – and made China look like a workers' paradise.

In 1957, believing that China was well under control and that the Communist Party enjoyed its citizens' full confidence, Mao invited what he expected would be praise and constructive criticism of the regime. With the familiar quotation from a Chinese classic "Let a hundred flowers bloom together and a thousand schools of thought contend!", he launched the ill-fated "Hundred Flowers" campaign. No one could have anticipated the result. The invitation to criticise the Party and the government performance was answered by an outpouring of pent-up frustration on the part of China's "intellectuals" (in other words, educated people with at least a high school education) who asked why, despite the obvious advances made in State enterprises, there had been such slow progress since 1949 in lifting the people out of their poverty and backwardness. They wrote to the press, went on strike, organised demonstrations, circulated anti-Party propaganda and attacked Party officials. No one was sacrosanct: not even the highest in the land. As criticism of the Party grew out of hand, a shocked Chairman, his prestige in tatters, struck back in a "rectification" campaign at those he called "stinking intellectuals" and "rightists". Anyone who had been rash enough to make criticisms faced "struggle" sessions at which the victims endured all kinds of violent abuse in order to extract confessions of guilt. Several million intellectuals – students, teachers, scientists, writers, lawyers and doctors – were consequently sent to labour camps to be re-educated by the peasants, many of them remaining unreleased until 1979. In this way, just at a time when the nation needed them most, some of the finest talents that the country possessed were wasted.

Following the humiliating experience of the Hundred Flowers campaign, Chairman Mao himself became impatient with the speed of economic progress; and that impatience led him to commit his second and more disastrous blunder. In the hope of achieving a "great leap forward" in production, in 1958 the country was hastily reorganised into 26,578 communes, with 123 million families suddenly finding themselves part of a vast military-style system of communes, brigades and production teams. Grasping for instant communism, Mao was determined to replace the individualism of the Chinese peasant with total collectivism, and so all private farm plots and free village markets were abolished as vestiges of capitalism.

Tragically for China, this stupendous, badly planned and mismanaged adventure coincided with three years of drought and other natural calamities, producing a famine so disastrous that, according to data released in Peking in 1980, twenty million people died of starvation. This largely man-made disaster forced Mao to step down from the office of state chairman in which he was succeeded by Liu Shaoqi, his nominated heir. China and Russia parted company in 1961, and the character of the communes was greatly modified, both private plots and free markets being restored. (Twenty-two years later, the communes would be virtually dismantled in favour of the "responsibility system" by which individual farmers would be held responsible for a given acreage of land, a move which has provided incentives for greatly increased production.) But the anti-rightist campaigns continued until by the end of 1965 forty million intellectuals and youth had been "sent down" to the country to engage in farm labour.

Mao was now planning his final gamble; the Great Proletarian Cultural Revolution. Its four main aims were to rebuild a Party totally loyal to himself, to make a clean break with China's bourgeois past through the elimination of the "four olds" (ideas, customs, culture and habits), to promote "continuous revolution" in each new generation and to purge the evil of "revisionism" (i.e. Marxism betrayed) as he saw it in Russia under Khruschev. If collectivism had been the watchword of the Great Leap Forward, then egalitarianism was to be that of the Cultural Revolution. The first target was what Mao regarded as the élitist educational system, and it was therefore the students who fired the "first volley of guns" in the most gigantic revolutionary fury since the Taiping Rebellion. As universities and schools were closed, students were recruited into the Red Guards and provided with armbands, Mao badges, the *Little Red Book* of quotations from Mao's speeches, free travel passes and free food and accommodation. They were ordered to fan out over the whole country "making revolution" and destroying the "four olds". Chanting "The East is Red", they shared an almost mystical veneration for Chairman Mao and treated the *Little Red Book* as a talisman having wellnigh magical powers. The walls of China's cities soon blossomed into a blaze of crimson "big character posters" which were used as a unique medium for political debate.

After nine tumultuous rallies in Peking where Chairman Mao personally reviewed fourteen million youth, the Red Guards set off "like a roaring swift current sweeping across thousands of miles" on an ideological rampage during which they created a fearful reign of terror and indulged in a ruthless vandalism of the nation's priceless treasures. With a fiendish delight in vicious cruelty and torture, they respected no one, not even the highest officials in the Communist Party. Intellectuals, regarded as guilty individuals, were therefore submitted to rituals of humiliation and violence of every kind. According to the *People's Daily*, during the decade beginning in 1966 a hundred million people (one in ten!) suffered political harassment. General Secretary Hu Yao-bang estimated that one million people had died and that thirty million had been persecuted during the Cultural Revolution, many of them being maimed for life as the result of severe beatings they received. As law and order broke down the opposing factions of Red Guards armed themselves and a madcap civil war began. But when three ultra-leftists in Shanghai whose patron was Mme Mao (Jiang Qing) – a group later to be dubbed the "Gang of Four" – attempted to arm the local militia and set up a Shanghai Commune, Chairman Mao, alarmed at the social rifts his revolution had caused, denounced the ultra-left anarchists and called in the People's Liberation Army under General Lin Biao to suppress all Red Guard activity.

Prominent Party members who became victims of the Cultural Revolution terror included Liu Shaoqi, who was denounced as the "Chinese Khrushchev" and stripped of all his offices. He died in solitary confinement in 1969, but eleven years later was posthumously rehabilitated and his honour officially restored – even to the extent of finding a place with Mao in the latter's mausoleum! The popular prime minister Zhou Enlai also lived under constant threat of attack, but thanks to Mao's protection he was able to save the country from total chaos and collapse. As the violence died down the colleges and schools were reopened, but eighteen million students of the "bourgeois" class, former Red Guards, now bitter at being manipulated and betrayed, were sent down to work on the farms. Their places were taken by semi-literate "worker-peasant-soldier" students. Thus education deteriorated to become mere political indoctrination and the study of the Thoughts of Mao Zedong.

The tragic loss of life during the Cultural Revolution, the "ten-year gap" in real education, the wholesale destruction of art treasures and the wasted natural resources add up to a disaster that defies imagination, a major catastrophe which reversed an entire period of China's development. Thus Mao's third blunder was the most damaging of all. This tragic drama was enacted behind a curtain of silence and the stark realities hidden from the outside world, even during President Nixon's historic visit to China in 1972.

In the winter of 1967–8, at the height of the Revolution, a party of about fifty students from Australia, a country regarded as friendly towards China, visited the People's Republic under the leadership of the only committed Christian in the group, Baden Teague, now a senator representing the state of Victoria. Teague was enthusiastic about what he had seen and experienced in conferences with Chinese student contemporaries. In 1967 he came to England to study for a PhD at Cambridge University and was introduced to me by the Australian Inter-Varsity Fellowship. I therefore arranged for him to show his fascinating slides of Cultural Revolution China at one of the Church House meetings. Very soon the two of us agreed to form a Christian China Study Group to meet several times a year in order to keep abreast of developments in that country particularly in relation to the Christian Church.

The first meetings attempted to analyse the distinctive features and emphasis of "Mao thought" such as "liberalisation" and "contradictions", and suggested possible Christian approaches to Marxist China. In 1969 what later proved to be a very accurate assessment of the Cultural Revolution was made. Books on China were regularly kept under review, and an investigation was undertaken into the quality of Christian broadcasts to China, aided by tape recordings of actual broadcasts and advised by a member of the BBC China section. This exercise bore fruit in the FEBC offices in Hong Kong. Experts also lectured on contemporary Chinese education and medicine.

The China Study Group continued its meetings with growing and enthusiastic support. Then in June 1971 it sent letters to the secretaries of the Asia committees of both the British Council of Churches (BCC) and the Evangelical Alliance (EA) urging them to call a meeting of all societies with an interest in China to consider what action might be possible should communication with the Church there be restored. Soon after this, in 1972, the BCC launched its own China Project with the financial backing of all the major denominations and invited the Revd Victor Hayward, a personal friend from my China days, to become project secretary. I was invited to join the extended committee.

That same year I accepted an invitation from German Church leaders to attend a conference on China near Frankfurt and to read a paper whose contents conflicted with the currently optimistic views about that country held by some of the world's "China experts" present. But there were also sympathetic German ears.

In 1974 a distinguished gathering of British Church representatives meeting in London under the auspices of the BCC was assigned the task of considering one of the themes propounded at the first of the "China studies" seminars held in Bastad, Sweden, the previous year: "The new man in the new China". These studies were sponsored by the Lutheran World Federation and the Roman Catholic Pro Mundi Vita. Most of those present were still starry-eyed about China, and one even expressed the opinion that what Britain needed was a Maoist revolution! P. R. Hensman, the able Singhalese author of a popular and controversial book on China entitled *Yellow Peril or Red Hope?* who was an enthusiastic protagonist of Maoist China was also among the invited participants. He in particular was highly indignant when Ralph Wang, a recent arrival from China, declared: "Don't confuse the model with the reality!"

"Ralph" (a pseudonym) Wang was a Christian and a Peking University graduate. He had taught in two universities and also worked on the staff of Peking Radio, where he had had access to classified information. He had been enmeshed in the entire Cultural Revolution drama and had finally left China in 1972. Wang went on to say: "All the propaganda out of China to which you have listened describes what China would like to be, the image she would wish to present to the world, the model at which she aims. But the reality falls far short of the model." There was in China no such thing as the totally selfless "new man" devoted to serving his fellow men, the mirage which had misled many in the West, said Mr Wang. I happened to be the only "evangelical" present, having been invited as the leader of the China Study Group and because the seminar wanted to hear an evangelical point of view. I took strong exception to some of the statements and findings of the Bastad seminar, and a few of those present endorsed my views.

In 1974 an international gathering of some seventy theologians met in Louvain, Belgium, to share their considered views about the Bastad papers. Almost unanimously the colloquium praised the achievements of Mao Zedong's regime in China as "a part of God's saving work in history", and even questioned whether Christianity was any longer essential to China! Dr Joseph Needham was quoted as equating current Chinese society with the Kingdom of God and describing China as "the only truly Christian country in the world"!

In 1977 I was again invited to attend a meeting of the

ecumenical China Studies Liaison Group in London, another in the long series of such gatherings held in Europe and North America following Bastad. A German professor who was a China expert had just returned from China and had witnessed in person the joy and relief that had followed the arrest and expulsion from the Communist Party of the notorious Gang of Four: the Chinese were calling this a "second Liberation". My views were heard sympathetically, as on previous occasions, by some of the Roman Catholics present, but no one else was yet prepared to "reverse their verdicts" (to use the Maoist jargon) and admit they had been seriously mistaken.

Ralph Wang assisted Victor Hayward in the China Project, and consequently, in the course of a year's close discussions and research, the latter's idealistic views were modified considerably. Hayward confessed that he had been far too naïve in accepting reports from China at face value and that he had not realised the gap there was between the ideals and the actual practice of Maoism. This, finally, became the majority position in the ecumenical world. Ralph Wang also lectured to the China Study Group, in illuminating fashion, on the subjects of Chairman Mao and the communes and education in China. While he was a guest in our home he shared hours of fascinating information about conditions in China as they really were.

At the end of 1970 the China Study Group made a summary of the first two years of meetings, in which it was acknowledged: "While we know little of the Church in China – at best a negligible minority – we may learn from their group fellowships, suffering and steadfastness." That ignorance was gradually dispelled in the following years.

For Christians the years after 1956 were increasingly painful. They had already suffered bitterly in the early period of the Revolution: now, many believers were numbered among the millions of "stinking intellectuals" banished to labour camps to suffer cruel tortures in the interest of ideological remoulding. They were sharing the lot of their non-Christian fellow citizens. Their survival under such treatment can only be explained by the fact that they, like Moses, endured as seeing Him who is invisible. Those leaders fortunate enough to escape exile had to endure intensified indoctrination. Then in 1958, on the grounds that missionaries had deliberately introduced denominationalism in order to keep control of the churches and thereby to perpetuate imperialist influence, the TSPM conducted a campaign to unite the churches – really a ploy to exert greater central control over them. But by 1960 the persecution of the churches as such had become so open and universal that most Christians harboured no further delusion about the promised religious freedom; even the TSPM had virtually ceased to function in anything but name and was helpless to defend the churches.

At this point, however, something very significant for the future took place. A Hong Kong newspaper, quoting statements from refugees reaching the colony after fleeing from the famine, reported that many Christians, weary of politically coloured and too-formal church services, were meeting in small, secret family groups, even at risk of punishment for breaking the law forbidding private assembly. In this way a sovereign God was already preparing His people for new patterns of church life in years to come. In 1964 the press renewed its attacks on religion, accusing church workers of using it as a cloak under which to hide their opposition to the government. Despite this increasing hostility churches in Zhejiang, Hunan and Shanxi continued to flourish through the early sixties. One northern leader declared: "In the past, the Church was built upon sand. Now it is being built on rock – THE Rock. God does not make mistakes!" Even in the capital Peking, according to a former university professor who before leaving China had been a member of one of the groups meeting secretly at considerable risk, there were many such family gatherings.

As the Cultural Revolution exploded in 1966, Christians immediately began to fear the implications of the elimination of the "four olds", "old cultures" clearly including religion. Since religious believers were among the "demons and mon-

sters" allegedly opposed to Mao, the Red Guards wasted
no time in seizing and closing church premises throughout
China, removing or defacing religious symbols and putting
the buildings to alternative use as schools, factories and
warehouses. Bibles, hymnals and other Christian literature
were confiscated and largely destroyed. What happened in
Amoy may be taken as an example. In the words of one
eye-witness:

> All church windows were smashed, the pews burned and
> the cross taken down. Every pastor was made to "walk
> the street" with a dunce's hat on his head and a placard
> around his neck announcing his crimes (a common prac-
> tice in humiliating intellectuals). One woman was beaten
> to death. Communist cadres and Red Guards searched
> every Christian home for Bibles, hymnals and other litera-
> ture. They then gathered over twenty YMCA and YWCA
> secretaries and forced them to kneel in front of the pile of
> burning books while a large crowd stood around observing
> the great spectacle. As the flames intensified and radiated
> their heat towards them, the victims cried out in excruciat-
> ing pain. It was a pitiful sight. Tormented by their excess-
> ive burns, most of them, including the general secretary
> of the YMCA, committed suicide by jumping from high
> buildings. Yet these men were the "progressive" secre-
> taries and pastors who had supported government policies
> in the 1950s and who had praised the Party for having
> attained what Christianity had failed to do in a hundred
> years! After this terrible ordeal, all church meetings in
> Amoy ceased.

The experience of the Amoy church was repeated throughout China to a greater or lesser degree. Not all copies of
the Scriptures were destroyed, but generally speaking the
Church became a Church without Bibles, without buildings
and without leaders, most of whom had been sent to labour
camps or prison where they were to remain for up to twelve
years. Christians were sometimes made to kneel in the

gutters to be mocked and spat upon, and some had had their heads shaved leaving hair in the shape of a cross as a "shameful identification". By Easter 1967 the liquidation of the entire organised Church was complete, and believers were forced to go underground and to gather in semi-secret family groups. Violent attacks on the churches continued. 1968 was the darkest and most difficult period of all, with persecutions intensifying, vile tortures being perpetrated and even the household meetings having to be suspended. Because university graduates were "intellectuals" the Christian students converted during the war and in the subsequent student revival now went to join the tens of thousands consigned to the political scrap-heap. Most of them were not rehabilitated until 1979, and even then, because of their history or family background, were kept under surveillance and given only menial tasks instead of the responsible ones for which their training qualified them. One doctor, a nominal Christian who was sent to a commune in Anhui to tend pigs, remembers with disgust going barefoot in the excrement and slurry of the sties and confesses that he often contemplated suicide. But among his fellow exiles was the Roman Catholic bishop Kung Pingmei, a devout man who by word and example eventually led him to a living faith in Christ. Another doctor, a lady who had returned from abroad to serve the new China only to have her home plundered and her parents killed and to suffer torture, described the Cultural Revolution as a thunderbolt that shattered a dream. Interestingly, it was only after she had lost everything that she found salvation in Christ.

Among other victims were students who had been involved in the post-war revival. "Stephen", my co-translator of Halley's *Bible Commentary* and one of our Peking student friends, later returned to that city with his new bride. But in 1955, as a leading member of the Christian Tabernacle congregation, he was arrested together with Wang Mingdao on a charge of sabotaging the TSPM and subjected to ideological brainwashing in prison. On his release two years later he returned to Shanghai to rejoin his family, only to be press-ganged in 1958, the year of the Great Leap Forward, into working in the communes. Labelled as a "counter-revolutionary", he was assigned to the bleak, cold north-western province of Gansu to work in a mine in the Yumen (Jade Gate) Mountains. There, during the great famine, he suffered from serious and chronic oedema or dropsy. He was therefore granted leave to rejoin his family for a rest. For nine years after that he lived the life of a coolie, making coal bricks and pulling a heavy goods cart around the streets. At the outbreak of the Cultural Revolution in 1966, as an "intellectual" and "counter-revolutionary", he again became a constant target for every form of humiliation, denunciation and abuse. But it was at that time that his three children were converted. In the winter of 1969, having suffered cruelly at the hands of the Red Guards and enduring a further period of separation from his family, he was "rusticated", along with his family, to north Jiangsu Province to be "reformed by labour". There, food shortages were acute and they had to live the rigorous, primitive life of farm labourers. As one of the "black elements", Stephen enjoyed no human rights until his rehabilitation in 1979.

"Henry", another member of the Student Christian Fellowship in Peking, had in 1956 gone on to qualify as a doctor and shown every sign of brilliance; but he too became victim of the anti-rightist and anti-intellectual campaigns in which some members of his profession were driven to suicide. Nevertheless, his outstanding skills as a research scientist enabled him to continue his medical career, though he was assigned to remote rural areas where he had to endure interminable hardships and privations. As a Christian, he continued to care lovingly for those who would otherwise have had no medical attention.

Hundreds like Stephen and Henry passed through these same deep waters of suffering and were treated as the scum of the earth, not because of any crimes they had committed but because of their loyalty to Christ and for His Name's sake. Now God has brought them out into a wealthy place of fruitful service for Himself.

It is significant that the early Church, when in the midst of persecution, quoted the second Psalm in its prayers. Beginning by calling on God as "Sovereign Lord" – sovereign in nature, in history and in grace – its members took courage from the assurance that the opposing forces, with all their threatenings, could only do "whatsoever Thy hand and Thy plan had predestined to take place". The Chinese Church must often have prayed this same prayer in the knowledge that God was inexorably fulfilling His purposes for the Chinese people and for the Church, both through them and through their enemies. Those early Christians knew, as Christians in China know today, that God reigns!

> While in affliction's furnace
> And passing through the fire,
> Thy love we praise, which tries our ways
> And brings us higher.
> We lift our hands exulting
> In Thy almighty favour;
> Thy love divine which made us Thine
> Shall keep us Thine for ever.
>
> *Charles Wesley*

14 The Cottage Meetings (1951–78)

"For dominion belongs to the Lord, and He rules over the nations."

Psalm 22:28

"The Church in China appears to have no future!" Such was the comment of an Indian Christian who attended the Ganefo Games in China in 1965. An English clergyman who visited China two years later found all churches closed and was unable to make any contact with Christians. Indeed, the decade of the Cultural Revolution, as far as the Christian Church was concerned, was a decade of silence. If the Indian visitor was thinking about traditional church structures, he was undoubtedly correct; but the true Church is not a man-made structure or a human organisation. Christians in China had discovered that even without Bibles, buildings or ordained ministers the community of the Holy Spirit is indestructible. God, who is never taken by surprise, always knows the end from the beginning and, in His sovereign wisdom, ensures the continuation of what He himself has initiated. "He that hath begun a good work in you will bring it to completion in the day of Jesus Christ," wrote the Apostle Paul to the Philippians from his prison cell.

God's survival tactic for His Church in China was what has been called the "cell group" church, which worships in a simple non-institutional fashion. As early as 1951 small groups of Christians, defying government restrictions, began to meet in secret and at irregular times. Subsequently, when normal church activities were suspended during the

Great Leap Forward these informal "cottage meetings" flourished again. And when in 1966 the demonic attack was launched against the Church and all its property confiscated, Christians courageously refused to contemplate defeat. At great risk to themselves and in the midst of one of the most terrible persecutions in history they persisted in meeting in their own homes to worship God and strengthen one another. Stripped of all the foreign trappings of the past, these groups, rooted in the home and protected by family loyalties, were finally dissociated from "Western imperialists". Deprived of hymnals, they sang – when safe to do so – portions of Scripture set to Chinese tunes, including among many others the well-known Twenty-Third Psalm and the Beatitudes. With no Bibles to read, members would share Scripture passages which they had previously committed to memory, whole chapters or even entire books of the New Testament sometimes having been "hidden in the heart". (Chinese memories are phenomenal!) They had only the Holy Spirit as their teacher. Testimonies to God's faithfulness, care and miracle-working power were exchanged joyfully for the mutual encouragement of everyone; but above all, prayer was offered without ceasing – sincere, fervent, believing prayer.

In many cases these cottage meetings declined to be called churches and preferred to be known simply as "fellowships". They shared a delightful simplicity and informality which Christians came to cherish, the members content to know Jesus as Lord whom they loved, served and proclaimed. Thus the Church, almost hidden from sight and in spite of the many difficulties and problems it faced, continued to grow.

The early Church, as already noted, prayed that in the face of threats Christians would continue to speak the Word with all boldness, while God would stretch out His hand to heal and perform signs and wonders through the Name of Jesus, in order to convince an unbelieving world of the truth. China's "underground" Christians prayed the same prayer, and God answered. As Communist officials, atheist cadres and many ordinary citizens suffering from chronic diseases experienced the healing touch of God in answer to the prayers of Christian groups which showed a loving concern, they too acknowledged the Living God and trusted Christ as Saviour. Not surprisingly, the authorities have, from the first, been at pains to deny all claims to miracles which atheists must regard as superstition: miracles do not fit in with a Marxist or materialist system!

As the trained pastors and church leaders were dragged off to prison or to labour camps, noble women often stepped into their places and became a key factor in church life; Mao Zedong rightly said, "Women hold up half the sky." In one city where there were forty cottage meetings women were the acknowledged leaders in most of them. When Mother Chang, a devout Christian, went to live in a small town knowing no one, she began to seek out other believers. Finding that they had not met for worship for three years, she opened a cheap "do-it-yourself" eating place for peasants coming to market. While downstairs all was bustle and conversation, the upstairs room was prepared for worship. One by one the believers arrived and the service began, Mother Chang sharing a simple Bible message drawn from her long experience. If the cry "Mother, we have run out of salt!" came up from below, it was a pre-arranged warning of danger; but the danger past, the service continued and Holy Communion was celebrated in great simplicity. Mother Chang came to know many Christians in the area to whom she was a true pastor; and as the believers witnessed to their friends and neighbours the little church grew steadily.

All over China faithful and courageous women like Mother Chang kept the fires of faith burning, encouraging the fearful and comforting the sorrowing. In one southern city, Christian women, contrary to known regulations, held a ten-week Bible school for seventy children. When one "intellectual" family was banished to the countryside an old Christian lady regularly told Bible stories to their children, with the result that both parents became Christians. But women also suffered for their faithfulness: many went to prison, and when prison became a fruitful place for witness to Christ they even asked to stay there! One woman had her head shorn eighteen times for publicly preaching the gospel. A seventy-year-old lady in Anhui who spent twenty-four years in prison now invites young believers to her home to be taught.

The loss of Bibles was a severe blow to people who treasured the Word of God, as so many Chinese Christians did. Yet not all Bibles were confiscated or destroyed by the Red Guards, and after the Cultural Revolution the Public Security Bureau sometimes returned quantities of them which they had kept in store. There are also stories of precious copies being hidden and saved from destruction – and happy the household church that had preserved even one Bible or New Testament! Such a copy would be passed around, each Christian keeping it for a week or two; or, in some cases, it would be taken to pieces and its pages circulated for copying or mimeographing. Christian radio stations also met the need by having the Bible read at dictation speed as, all over China, listeners with one ear glued to their transistor sets wrote down passage after passage of the Scriptures. (One elderly doctor copied out the entire Bible twice!) At one time, before Bibles had again become more easily available, there may have been more handwritten portions of Scripture than printed ones, Bibles being as rare as diamonds.

In a certain work unit responsible for felling timber and floating the logs down a mighty river, the workers all knew each other intimately, eating and sleeping together. One of the men was a Christian who had a copy of the New Testament and Psalms which had been given to him by a visiting relative. As his work involved getting quite wet frequently, he used to wrap the precious book in plastic for protection. One morning, long before the others had stirred, he went into the forest to read the Scriptures; but hearing footsteps and fearing being caught with his Bible he put the book back in his pocket and pretended to be taking an early morning walk. Unfortunately, the unexpected visitors knew him, searched his pockets, found the New Testament and asked him if he had risen early specially to read the book. "Yes," he replied, rather fearful of the consequences, only to discover that the men knew someone else in the camp who had a similar book which he read openly, and that that was how they had recognised it. This information made the secret believer think, and he too began to read the New Testament openly while sitting on his camp cot. To his surprise, two other men came over and joined him, one with a complete Bible and one with a Gospel of Mark; and together the three became the nucleus of a Bible study group in the commune. So the Living Word lived on in China.[1]

But Bibles were not the only loss during the Cultural Revolution: commentaries and Bible-reading aids had also been destroyed. One of the cottage meetings in Shanghai therefore produced its own outline of Christian doctrine and practice to help its members, entitled *Ten Main Points and Seven Points for Every Day*. A simple farmer who came to know Christ in 1962 through the witness of a cottage meeting, on being given a copy of the Bible began to study it diligently. His wife, who was not a Christian, feared for the safety of the family should her husband's work on the outline be discovered, and destroyed drafts of the manuscript on five occasions. But in the end she too was converted, and eventually the manuscript was completed and 10,000 copies mimeographed and distributed. Pastors released from prison in 1978 examined it and warmly approved of it; and in recognition of the farmer's work they ordained him at a simple service in his own village. It is probable that most of the potential Bible teachers trained in China's many Bible and theological colleges were detained in prison or labour camps until their release and "rehabilitation" in 1979; but in their absence God raised up humble people both in the cities and in the villages, like the farmer who wrote his Bible handbook, to preserve the truths of His Word and to teach others.

In addition to their simple forms of worship and love for

the Bible, these secret Christians enjoyed a reputation for their love for one another and for the joy and peace they manifested in the midst of suffering which amazed their neighbours. They were also well known for their loving care for all those in need or trouble. In the Cultural Revolution many people lost everything they possessed, and it was the Christians who shared their own food and clothing with the needy and the poor, especially with those whose bread-winners had been killed or thrown into prison. They visited the bereaved and the suffering to bring them comfort. When one Communist schoolteacher became very seriously ill it was the Christians who did all they could to care for her in her illness, so that when she recovered she too accepted Christ, only to suffer public ridicule on return to duty. Required to appear at a public "confession" meeting, she protested: "When I was ill, you did nothing to help me. It was the Christians who did everything!" – a truth which shamed and silenced her critics. Numerous instances of this kind made a deep impression on non-Christians.

A Christian lady from overseas returned to China in 1974, following the worst fury of the Cultural Revolution, to visit her native village, fearful of what she might find. In fact she discovered eighty rejoicing believers with a strong, pure faith for which some had been sent to prison, where they had continued witnessing to the other prisoners. In that village, prayer and fasting were normal activities and God was demonstrating to a sceptical world His power to heal. A Singapore businessman with no Christian background returned to China in 1975 to visit relatives and found, to his astonishment, that they had all been converted to Christianity; through their witness he too found the Saviour. A nominal Christian who visited China found her relatives even stronger believers as a result of the suffering they had endured, and their testimony caused her to exchange a nominal profession for a genuine faith in Christ.

But the Church paid a heavy price for its survival, and the full tale of suffering has not yet been told. The vicious torture, cruel beatings (some to death), rapes and lootings at the hands of the wild, ruthless and undisciplined Red Guards had been beyond description. Many outstanding Christians who had escaped earlier imprisonment at the time of the Hundred Flowers episode and the anti-rightist campaigns of the sixties went to prison, where they were to remain for a further twelve years, leaving wives and children without support. In the face of threats and demands to renounce their faith and under fearful pressures, there were, sadly, those who weakened and yielded: in this grim warfare spiritual casualties were not uncommon. But for those who endured, faith was wonderfully strengthened. As St. Peter wrote: "In this you rejoice, though now for a little while, you may have to suffer various trials so that the genuineness of your faith, more precious than gold which, though perishable, is tested by fire, may redound to praise and honour at the revelation of Jesus Christ." Certainly, the hope of Christ's return was one of the major factors which sustained suffering believers as they passed through the valley of deep darkness. Listen to the voice of one such sufferer: "So many Christians have died already . . . I was one of the 'evil spirits and wicked devils' deceiving the people with religion . . . I had to carry placards and stand in the street to be mocked. We Christians were a laughing stock . . . I was imprisoned, then sentenced to hard labour . . . But the suffering I endured was so much less than Jesus bore." Another wrote to a friend: "In these twenty years, I would say that the Chinese Church has not so much suffered for the Lord: rather it has been purified by the Lord . . . May the lessons we learned in those years call out a people who walk in the fear of the Lord!"

These sufferers have proved the truth of the saying "The hotter the crucible, the more refined the Church!" They regarded suffering as a glorious and essential privilege to be desired, not avoided: not "something strange", in the words of St. Peter. One lady in exile in north-west China wrote: "The myrrh of my suffering is the only gift I have to offer to my Saviour!" Given that the New Testament epistles were written in the midst of persecution and suffering, the hidden Church in China had much in common with the early Church, even sharing an experience similar to that of the church in the catacombs during the Roman terror; its members knew from experience the strength which derives from weakness and the "power of powerlessness". As Jonathan Chao has said: "Christians in China interpret the last thirty-four years of prolonged suffering as a gift of God's profound grace to the Chinese Church to cleanse her from her impurities, to test the genuineness of their faith and loyalty, to train them for obedience and progress unto greater maturity, and to enable them to gain a deeper experience with Christ." The question of why, if God loves the Chinese Church, he allows it to suffer does not arise; but one observer has said: "If God loves the American (or British) Church so much, why doesn't He allow us to suffer so that our churches might be purified, our faith strengthened and our relationship with Christ deepened to serve Him whole-heartedly?"

At this point it is important to make a distinction between the mature Christians who were called to pass through the fearful Cultural Revolution (House Churches Mark 1) and those innumerable new Christians who have come into the Church since 1978 (House Churches Mark 2). The former were, for the most part, the older, well-grounded Christians of the pre-revolution years. The cottage meetings of the Cultural Revolution period were necessarily small, family-based and largely secret, giving little hint of the phenomenal growth yet to come. In the fiery kiln of suffering God was preparing His vessels for future use, and those comparatively small family or cottage meetings were to become springboards for the tremendous "leap forward" in conversions after 1978: to change the metaphors, the early cottage meetings were a solid bridgehead for a major advance against the powers of darkness in China and launching pads for a spectacular explosion of Holy Spirit power. Until about 1976 the world knew virtually nothing of the existence of those numerous semi-secret home fellowships.

In 1975 Brother Andrew, *"God's Smuggler"*, arranged an international conference in Manila, Philippines, called the

"Love China Seminar", to which I and other fellow workers of the Overseas Missionary Fellowship were invited as speakers. At the opening gathering the convenor urged the conference not merely to discuss the problems but to reach conclusions as to what action must be taken to bring aid to China's beleaguered Christians. Chinese speakers and missionaries who had served in China then provided the background information about the Chinese Church as they had known it. Experts lectured on Marxism and Maoism and, as far as possible, updated the assembly as to current developments on China's Mainland; though, as already mentioned, little was then known about the state of the Church. Bible studies directed our minds to the Word of God and God's purposes for His Church, while prayer and intercession were given first priority. Discussion groups tried to grapple with the problems of China's future and of that of the Church there, but clearly in 1975 the time for action had not come. Chairman Mao still lived; and with the Gang of Four holding high office the Chinese nation remained in the firm grip of the ultra-leftists, who, even as we met, were plotting to seize power just as soon as Mao, then a very sick man, should die.

As the conference drew to a close it was apparent that little or nothing could be done immediately towards bringing aid to China's Christians. But if present action was still out of the question, prayer would prepare the way for future action. Every one of the 200 participants, therefore, including myself, returned to their home countries in four continents with a strong determination to mobilise prayer for China on a world-wide scale. In Britain, this pledge was discharged in the "China – Too Hard for God?" campaigns which were held all over the country during 1976 and 1977, as a result of which hundreds of British Christians took up the burden of prayer for China and the Church there. The timing was critical: a sovereign God was about to display His power!

15 "A Hundredfold" (1978–83)

> "And He who sat upon the throne said, 'Behold I
> make all things new.'"
>
> *Revelation 21·5*

The story of one unusual church, told by one of its members,
spans the whole period from 1949 to the present day:

This is a mining town, and we are some of the finest
miners in the country. We hope our church is a good
church. We belong to it, love it and want to share the
Gospel with others. Everyone in town knows we are
Christians and that on Sundays we gather for worship in
the morning at ten, and, for those who have to go down
the pits, in the evening. Out of four thousand miners and
families, three hundred and forty-six, at the last count,
are members of the church. We are small in number, but
you would never guess it if you came into this place on
Sunday. You would think the whole town is Christian
with people carrying Bibles and nodding to one another
and smiling. Brother Tang is an extraordinary person,
big and vigorous and, though in his sixties, never seems
to tire. He began as a young man working in the pits,
gradually moving up to the rank of supervisor. He has
education, including a year studying theology at college.
Then, so he told us, he had to quit because his father was
forced by something or somebody to leave the city. So he
settled in and became a miner. This was immediately
before the "Liberation" in 1949. In the mine he got a

Bible study going. The times were chaotic. Brother Tang soon got into trouble with the management and was put in gaol several times. But the union always got him out. It had to because he was one of their leaders . . . We are fairly well informed of what is going on elsewhere. I think we could have a pastor, but then we have Brother Tang, who is more than a pastor to us . . . We now have our own Bibles. I suppose almost every family possesses one. We share no Bibles in common. The most difficult period was 1968 when the Red Guards were against religion and against Bibles. So our church went without Bibles for two or three years and our people were circulating pages of the Bible. It was a sad and difficult time.[1]

Such is the story of one church, a growing church, a church matured through suffering. Who could have believed when the missionaries sorrowfully left China in 1951 that a Protestant Church then numbering fewer than one million in the space of thirty years would have multiplied many times over? This extraordinary phenomenon, other than being a sovereign activity of God, needs explanation.

1976 was crisis year for China. First the highly respected premier, Zhou Enlai, died; then Zhu De, the veteran marshal of the Red Army; and finally, the revered Chairman Mao Zedong himself. Each was mourned by a nation whose destiny was suddenly placed in the balance. Anticipating the Chairman's death, the Gang of Four had been plotting the coup which would give them supreme power; but that coup failed, and all four Gang members were arrested and eventually tried for their towering crimes. Their arrest as the end of a disastrous rule was hailed with intense relief.

With Hua Guofeng succeeding briefly as Chairman and also as prime minister, a new day seemed to be dawning; but it was Deng Xiaoping, the former dynamic Party secretary who, as Hua's successor, would institute a radical programme to speed up the modernisation of China. Deng secured the appointment to the posts of Party secretary (the office of chairman had been abolished) and prime minister of two able younger men, Hu Yaobang and Zhao Ziyang, both of whom were fully behind him in his determination to destroy the ultra-left faction associated with the Gang of Four and to press forward with the "four modernisations" (agriculture, industry, science and defence). Deng constantly emphasised the importance of the United Front within which all sections of the national life must work together towards a common goal. He was anxious to include the Christian churches because they had earned approval for their opposition to the Gang during the Cultural Revolution. God's reign in the kingdom of men is often seen when He removes evil men from power and promotes others to take their places, as in the instance of the Gang of Four: "It is God who executeth judgement, putting down one and lifting up another" (Psalm 75:1); "It is He who . . . brings princes to nought and makes the rulers of the earth as nothing" (Isaiah 40:23).

After the traumatic events of 1976 the atmosphere all over China underwent a marked change. The authorities became more tolerant towards religion, and Christians began to enjoy greater liberty than they had known for twenty years, becoming increasingly bold in their witness. They were no longer afraid of worshipping openly in their family gatherings or of summary arrest. They look back to 1977 as the year when the Church experienced God's care and mercy in a special way. In 1979 many Christians were released from labour camps after their long detention.

Very significantly, there developed at this same time a profound revulsion against the Cultural Revolution and a growing criticism of those who had been behind it. The *Little Red Book* and the Mao badges were discarded, the statues and portraits of the Chairman disappeared, and a slow process of "demaoisation" followed throughout the nation. The manifest failure of Marxism to raise China out of her backwardness and poverty had left a spiritual vacuum in the hearts of the people, especially young intellectuals. Articles in leading Chinese newspapers admitted that the nation was undergoing a crisis of faith. Professor Audrey

Donnithorne, an acknowledged authority on Chinese politics, wrote, "People are yearning for faith in a new absolute!" And Paul Kauffman of Hong Kong said: "China, in the vacuum of a lost faith, is now more ready for a true spiritual awakening than it has ever been in its long history. There is a hunger for a faith beyond the grasp of the state." There was no doubt about the vacuum, and young people in particular felt depressed and empty. But their hearts and minds were, by these means, being prepared for the Good News. As one listener wrote to the Far East Broadcasting Company (FEBC):

> In the year since my graduation, my soul has been constantly wandering as in a graveyard. Hatred, despair, distress and uncertainty mingle in my mind all day long. I ask myself whether there is a god to make me wiser, lead me towards the light, release me from my distress and the pursuit of the devil so that I can gain spiritual freedom and joy. What you preach today is about God who is able to set me free from hell! But what is God? In fact, is there a God existing in this world?

One estimate is that more than half of China's population, that is 500 million, are under twenty years of age! These young people have had a specially raw deal, being the victims of ten years of tumult. The generation of the Red Guards is a lost one whose confidence in their earlier political views has been shattered. Teenagers born during the Cultural Revolution are said to lack a social conscience or a sense of higher purpose and are bewildered and dispirited about the future. For ten years after 1966 they had no opportunity for a normal education, and high school graduates still felt frustrated that university education was available to only about 3–4% of those eligible; the rest had no choice of career but were assigned by the Party to tasks in industry, agriculture or administration, ill-equipped as they were for the rush for modernisation. They were bitter at the exploitation and dissipation of their youthful energies, and

in the winter of 1978–9 the simmering discontent and disillusionment boiled over as millions of words pasted up on
the "democracy wall" at Xidan in Peking suggested possible
alternatives to Marxism and demanded genuine democracy
and human rights. Dissident newspapers went on sale and
were quickly bought. But all too soon this new freedom of
expression became too free for the Politburo's liking and
Deng Xiaoping brought the "Peking Spring" to a summary
end. Poster-writing on the wall was forbidden; and one of
the leading dissidents was arrested, brought to trial and
sentenced to fifteen years' imprisonment as a warning to
others.

In 1982 the government again clamped down on such
freedom as there had been, imposing stricter regulations in
the universities and more intense indoctrination on the
students. But China's youth, in spite of the surface cynicism,
is deeply concerned about the country's future. They are a
sceptical, thoughtful and enquiring generation searching for
answers to the meaning of life and the secret of true happiness. A former Red Guard, now a journalist in Hong Kong,
believes that even though public expression by the democracy movement has been silenced the Cultural Revolution
generation are now the real leaders of China's thought and
will have an important role in the nation's future. Youth is
a staggering problem for China's leaders, who know that it
is also their country's hope. Amidst all these problems young
people, in their disillusionment with Marxism and Maoism,
are turning to Christ in huge numbers and showing extraordinary courage and zeal.

Christian youth is also the hope of the Christian Church.
Christian young people have suffered even more grievously
than their non-Christian contemporaries, facing discrimination in education and being assigned to the most menial
occupations regardless of their capabilities. The government
has issued repeated warnings against the teaching of religion
to minors under the age of eighteen, and if young people
attend church (in spite of the Constitutional opposition to
all discrimination on the grounds of religion) they are often

reported to their work units by guards posted at the church doors and subsequently penalised.

The long, anxious silence about the Church since 1966 was first broken in 1971, the year when, after years of isolation from the rest of the world, Zhou Enlai decided to open China's doors to the world again by inviting the USA to send a team of table-tennis players to China. "Ping-pong diplomacy" was the prelude to a personal visit to Peking and Shanghai by the American president himself, a visit which culminated in the "Shanghai Communiqué" promising an early restoration of diplomatic relations between the two nations. A year after President Nixon's visit in 1972, the Chinese Government opened a single place of worship in Peking as a concession to the wishes of the diplomatic corps. The appointed clergy were all Chinese, but only a small handful of their fellow countrymen ventured to join the Westerners in worship. So much for the background to the sudden bursting forth of spiritual life in the late seventies.

The first news of the real Chinese Church for nearly six years burst on the world in 1973, exciting all who heard it. Since the 1966 Cultural Revolution all churches in Fuzhou, the provincial capital of Fujian Province and one of the treaty ports, had been closed. Secret family worship had, however, been maintained, and these fellowships grew in number until in 1971 the arrest of leading members forced the meetings to be suspended. But it was then that God acted and visited His people with His quickening Spirit, and hundreds, mostly young people, again began to meet in private homes.

By 1973 a Christian community numbering over 1,000 had grown up, and it was this thrilling news which cheered all who had been praying for China and her Christians. The authorities, alarmed by the large number of Christians, then ordered the meetings to cease. In 1974 five leaders were arrested, paraded in dunces' caps and imprisoned. On their release these men and women bravely continued their pastoral visiting, and the number of believers multiplied dramatically. By 1980 Bishop Peter Hsieh of Fuzhou, whose predecessor had been tortured to death, was able to report a community of 20,000 Christians in this single city of a million people! On one of his pastoral journeys the bishop had found 7,000 new Christians in seven remote mountain villages being taught by two elderly workers. The church in Fujian was clearly growing much faster than in the days when the missionaries had been present. Two congregations of 2,000 each were worshipping every Sunday at the Flower Lane Church in Fuzhou, half of them being young people. "They are thirsty for something spiritual," the bishop reported, "and they appreciate long sermons!"

In 1981 the Fuzhou leaders conducted a two months' course for forty or more voluntary lay workers. In 1980, Christians throughout the whole province were known to number at least 600,000 and in that same year, in one area alone, 6,000 new believers were baptised. One lady who had been travelling around the province preaching and teaching God's Word was arrested and put into gaol. There she went on hunger strike, and when moved to hospital she led another patient, the wife of a Communist cadre, to Christ. Christians were, in fact, appearing in the most unlikely places – even within Communist Party ranks and in the Youth League. This caused an angry press to renew its attacks on religion and to emphasise the total incompatibility between Christianity and Marxism.

Adjoining Fujian to the north is the "favoured province" of Zhejiang, where even more sensational news was soon to reach the outside world. In 1980 a young third-generation Christian who under political indoctrination had rejected the faith of his parents and had then rediscovered Christ for himself, paid a visit to Hong Kong. There he reported the almost incredible news that in his native county of Wenzhou, the city where the church had first been planted by the one-legged Stott, there were now 50,000 Christians or one in eight of the population meeting in up to 600 household gatherings. Only one eighty-year-old pastor had survived the early carnage, and he had spent twenty years in prison. It had all begun during the Cultural Revolution, when the church leaders had called for three months of prayer and fasting. Small meetings had been resumed in 1967, but this had provoked intensified opposition and fierce persecution. Christians had been humiliated, tortured, threatened and subjected to "struggle" sessions. Many had died in prison, while others had been either killed or crippled by savage beatings. The survivors, however, had emerged as powerful disciple-makers, although sometimes the only kind of public witness possible had been at well-attended Christian funerals where full advantage had been taken to proclaim a living Saviour and a living hope; even so, the funeral organisers had often been arrested. In about 1978, a powerful work of the Holy Spirit began bringing to Christ men and women in their thousands, including large numbers of young people. The growth was prolific, and renewed persecution failed to quench the fires of revival; even children remained true to their Lord despite constant threats from their teachers. On one occasion 500 church leaders attended a retreat in a Christian village, one of their tasks being to compile a manual of discipleship.

But it was not only in the Wenzhou district that the Holy Spirit was at work; Zhejiang Province has a long record of many very live churches or assemblies associated with missions or with the "Little Flock". After 1978, cottage meetings again began to multiply throughout the province, some starting in a small way but others, like the one in a village with 1,000 believers, growing to large dimensions. In one mountain region of 10,000 people one in three of the population had become Christians, meeting in fifteen church centres. Ten leaders were travelling from place to place expounding the Scriptures and instructing new believers, the services often lasting for four hours! A China Bible Seminary graduate who travels throughout the province teaching both old and new believers makes a practice of inviting two representatives from each house church to attend a week of meetings; so if 200 people arrive the indication is that there are at least 100 meeting-places in that one area. In some communes the majority of the members are Christian, and in one commune of 10,000 people which is totally Christian the commune officials have named the production teams "Jesus Team No. 1, Jesus Team No. 2" and so on and even advised other communes to "emulate the Jesus teams", which have regularly reached high production levels.

In some rural areas over 90% of the population are Christian – a totally unprecedented statistic in the history of the Church in China. One church which used to hold retreats and training classes for young converts in the nearby mountains in 1975 baptised 100 people in a mountain stream. Militiamen dispatched to prevent the baptisms thought they saw soldiers surrounding the Christians and so withdrew their detachment in the belief that the army had the matter under control; but there were no soldiers, and the baptismal service proceeded without any interference! One semi-official estimate is that in Zhejiang alone there may be as many as five million Christians.

Further north still from Zhejiang lies yet another coastal province, Jiangsu, through which the Changjiang (Yangzi) River flows and pours into the sea near Shanghai. Other famous cities along its course are the former capital Nanjing, Yangzhou (where Marco Polo was once the mandarin) and Zhenjiang. Wuxi is a great industrial centre, and Suzhou is paired with Hangzhou for their charm and beauty. Shanghai has again become the focus of attention because in that city, where the Cultural Revolution raged most fiercely, there are now over one million believers. During the 1982 Christmas period over 4,000 house groups held special meetings in addition to the celebrations in the open churches. In Nanjing, too, believers are both numerous and active. Suzhou, with a population of 600,000, has many Christians. Elsewhere, on one Sunday alone, a seventy-year-old pastor preached in a tent to a gathering of 500 in the morning and to 1,000 in the evening. In one "People's Commune" the secretary of a Party committee was converted and gave up his influential position and membership of the Party to become a preacher, leading many to Christ. Everywhere there is rapid church growth. As the old pastor said: "The fire of the Gospel has been lit and it is going to keep on burning like a prairie fire!"

Turning south again to yet another coastal province, we reach Guangdong with its well-known cities of Canton and Swatow, both among the original "treaty ports". Canton has, naturally, been influenced by its proximity to Hong Kong and by the thousands of Chinese from there who visit the city and other places in the provinces at special seasons. It is here that most Bibles and other items of Christian literature enter China, an activity which creates great problems both for the government and for Christians. Large numbers have turned to Christ in recent years, in Canton itself and in the rural areas. A great spiritual awakening has occurred there: in one small town a church of only 100 members actually baptised 300 converts or three times its own membership, and in one provincial university 200 students regularly meet for Bible study. In Swatow, north from Canton, where the church suffered so severely in 1966, membership has grown to 500, up to 80% of whom are young people.

Hainan Island off the south-west coast of Guangdong and Guangxi Provinces is an idolatrous place. But even here the Church is growing apace, in spite of the persecution of the fifties and sixties when many pastors were murdered. Today, Christians are found all over the island meeting in many house fellowships.

It is not surprising that the first reports of renewed Christian activities after the calamitous Cultural Revolution should have come from the coastal provinces, for it was there, in the treaty ports, that Christianity first took root and the first churches were planted. Third- and fourth-generation Christians might thus be expected to weather the storms of persecution more successfully than others. At first it seemed unwise to generalise on the basis of the encouraging situation in these provinces; in the absence of news from the inland provinces, it could not be assumed that the remarkable religious revival taking place in the east of China was occurring elsewhere. But then tourists passing through Henan discovered, almost by accident, that the spiritual "explosion" was by no means confined to the coastal provinces. A ninety-year-old pastor who, after being shot in the legs by the Red Guards, had become permanently bedridden, wrote to Hong Kong asking if he might "borrow" a Bible should Bibles be in short supply there also! His own Bibles and library had been totally destroyed in 1966; yet here he was, the pastor of over 5,000 baptised Christians in twenty local churches. With tears in his eyes he told the visitors how the greatest turning to the Lord in his entire ministry had occurred during the previous two years, and that the converts included many young people. This old pastor, without the aid of Bibles or other books, had been training men of reputation and experience to be his successors in the leadership. The stories told of past suffering had been heart-rending, but tales of God's miracle-working power had been equally thrilling. This first renewed contact with Western Christians was celebrated in a worship and testimony meeting, 200 people crowding into and around the pastor's home. Finally, a consignment of Bibles – not just one to borrow! – was delivered and received with deep emotion and thanksgiving to God.

And this story is no exception. All over this province with its population of seventy million people, mostly farmers, astounding numbers have been turning to the Lord: whole villages or production teams at a time. A Christian girl told a traveller, "Many, many beyond our imagination are turning to Christ!" In one county alone, in a population of 700,000, Christians number 300,000, and they are actively supporting witness teams spreading the Good News. A young Christian from Canton who paid a visit to south Henan found "meeting points" in almost every village and was impressed by the godliness, the trusting faith and the Bible knowledge which characterised those groups. A blind itinerant evangelist has found whole households and even whole villages newly rejoicing in Christ; one city has even been called a "Jesus nest" by hostile cadres, the number of

Christians there being so great. Said one pastor: "It is God who is mightily at work today! We are doing nothing." That very morning he had already baptised 114 people, a typical weekly event for him. It has been estimated that in recent years throughout the province up to 3,000 baptisms may have been taking place every day of the year, and in all these groups young people were in the majority; in one city they have formed their own youth choir. Knowledgeable observers believe there may be as many as ten million Christians in this, China's second most populous province. Thus it is scarcely surprising that the government is not a little disturbed and has ordered special surveillance of the churches there and imposed severe restrictions on Christian gatherings, on listening to foreign Christian radio stations and on the movements of evangelists from one area to another.

If the most remarkable church growth has been taking place in Fujian, Zhejiang and Henan Provinces, all the other provinces have equally been experiencing unprecedented growth: from the barren, remote steppes of Mongolia to the high mountains and deep ravines of south-west China; from the oases of central Asia to the rich rice-growing region of central China; from Peking to Canton and from Chongqing to Shanghai. For example, in inner Mongolia, a notorious dumping ground for political unwanteds and where, sadly, many Christians have died or failed to return from labour camps, conversions have multiplied and the seed of God's Word has taken root and borne fruit. One area has twelve groups, each with about eighty believers attending; one entire production team, including the leading cadre, was Christian. A lady who was separated from her husband, a banished intellectual, for seventeen years and was herself chained, beaten, starved, paraded and forced to work long hours, eventually started a Bible class which has since grown remarkably. Christians released from prison have often returned to find churches revived and flourishing with up to 100 people at each cottage meeting. Groups of Christians in the cities have been known to sing hymns on the busy streets, and some are reaching out to the Mongol population with the gospel. In one area where there are forty cottage meetings and 1,200 believers, baptismal services are held every Sunday and on public holidays. Even "rusticated" Red Guards have shown themselves to be open to the gospel.

At China's other extremity, in the mountain ranges of the south-west, tour guides who, in answer to tourists' questions, often profess ignorance about the presence of churches, freely acknowledge the existence of large Christian communities among the "minority" tribes. Of the present believers 95% have been converted since 1976, and there are ten times as many Christians today as there were in 1949. In one county alone where previously there had been only 400 Christians there are now 80,000. Christians among the Lisu and Miao are said to number 100,000 and their religion is officially described by the Chinese authorities as "Christian". Their "chapel" is often a huge limestone cavern holding as many as 2,000 worshippers.

A Lisu Christian who returned from Burma, whither he and thousands of his tribe had escaped in the early fifties, found thirty flourishing churches in the Salween Valley, where 7,000 converts had been baptised in two years. Bibles were in such short supply that in one place the sole precious volume was kept hidden beneath rocks in a mountain cave away from the eyes of the authorities; only selected leaders knew of its whereabouts and in their free time went to read it before concealing it again carefully. Not far away, a Chinese pastor had spent many years in a labour camp in which there had been many "minority" Tibetans whom he had befriended and whose language he had learnt. At the end of ten years, through his witness, fifty of them believed the gospel and on their release were baptised in a cold mountain lake. This is thought to have been the largest number of Tibetans ever to have been baptised at one time.

In the far north-west thousands have believed in Chinese Turkestan or Xinjiang Province; and in Urumqi, the provincial capital, several hundred believers meet for worship in seven or eight households. In another town it is reported that 120,000 new converts meet in 330 separate venues, many having been converted through the radio. How the veteran George Hunter and the Trio of inveterate ladies or even the young pioneers of 1932 would rejoice if they could return today! Gansu, Qinghai, Ningxia and Shaanxi all report a tremendous upsurge in the numbers of believers, with seventy household churches in Xian, the Shaanxi capital, alone and attended by several thousand Christians. Converts are numbered in their thousands, and one church not far from Xian baptised 7,000 in two years. Lanzhou, China's second industrial city, where my colleague of Luan days is still serving as a pastor (and has twice sent his greetings by tourists), has 90,000 Christians, while Xining, capital of Qinghai, has thirty house groups.

In Sichuan, China's most populous province and major rice-bowl, where during the Cultural Revolution workers in the capital Chongqing once fought one another with machine-guns, artillery and tanks, many cottage meetings are known to exist, in the city and also the rural areas, and Christians have been travelling thousands of miles from their base on evangelistic journeys. Sailing down the Changjiang (Yangzi) River through the spectacularly beautiful gorges and past the equally spectacular Gedzou Dam, which, with three additional dams to be constructed within the gorges, will eventually supply China with 30% of her power needs one comes to the central provinces of Hubei, Hunan, Anhui and Jiangxi. In Hubei, Christians in some communes are numbered in thousands and even tens of thousands, while in neighbouring Anhui, a strong Maoist stronghold, at least 70,000 are known to have turned to Christ. A visitor to Jiangxi found 5,000–6,000 new believers in just four large villages; and everywhere in this province, where in 1927 Mao established his first "soviet" and where there have been many martyrs, including eight in the Cultural Revolution, astounding numbers of converts are reported. One city has 120,000 believers and another 70,000. One town had no building big enough to hold everybody, so that over 2,000

worshippers gathered at night on the deserted motor highway to sing and pray and listen to visiting preachers.

Pursuing the journey down the river to Shanghai, it will
be found that though fifteen or so church buildings have been
reopened for worship at least 1,000 small family fellowships
continue to meet in spite of TSPM instructions to disband
and attend the open churches. In about 1981, Christians
began to hold open-air meetings in the city parks; the
meeting on the site of the old racecourse was one of the
largest known public gatherings and became a rallying point
for Christians from all over China and an opportunity for
the exchange of news. In 1982 the authorities banned these
meetings.

Shandong Province on the north-east coast has associations with the True Jesus Church, the Jesus Family and
the revivals of the 1930s among the Southern Baptists.
The churches there, as elsewhere, have been experiencing
tremendous growth, and cottage meetings have multiplied.
In Jinan, the provincial capital, there are reported to be
20,000 believers. In the picturesque port city of Qingdao
over 1,000 Christians attend Sunday worship, and in Yantai
(Chefoo) over 600. One leader said: "God really is among
us! The time is ripe for Him to reveal His glory!"

Going further north to Shanxi, the martyr province, "innumerable" people are reported as turning to Christ: in the
north as many as 3,000 believed through listening to gospel
broadcasts. But in Peking cottage meetings have been few
and those very private; Christian witness there is difficult.
In the country around the capital, however, many Christians
are boldly witnessing and working for God. In southern
Hebei very large numbers have believed, and in spite of
intensified persecution extensive evangelistic journeys are
resulting in many conversions.

What has been happening, especially since 1978 when the
churches began to enjoy a period of toleration, has been like
a forest fire sweeping over China, every spark setting another
tree alight – a glorious conflagration! "Never in one hundred years of Gospel presentation has there been such a

widespread response to Christianity as today," Paul Kauffman of Hong Kong has claimed. The impossible is happening as Party members, even Party secretaries, commune
officials, Communist cadres and Youth League members
join the new believers. A neighbourhood Party boss recently
accepted a Bible from a visitor and, in the presence of a
BBC correspondent, commented: "You don't know it, but
Christianity is spreading rapidly in China because people
are disillusioned with Communism!"

Not surprisingly, these dramatic developments have
drawn the fire of the national press, which goes out of its
way to criticise religion. Marxism believes that under its
scientific system and with proper education religion will
ultimately wither away – so when Party members begin to
turn to Christianity, panic sets in! The press has gone out
of its way to emphasise that no one can be a religious believer
and a Party member at one and the same time; indeed, it
was this situation which led to the 1982 government Statement on Religion, directed almost solely at Christianity.

We have already considered some of the causes of this
extraordinary turning away from Marxism to religious faith,
but how it has happened needs further explanation. Evangelism, as known in the West, consists largely of campaigns,
crusades, rallies and missions. But none of these activities
is possible under a Communist government; so how have
these multitudes of people become Christians, if not through
evangelistic services? The answer must be that it has been
by encountering people who know the secret of peace of
heart and are willing to share that secret. During the Cultural
Revolution the Church became identified with "the people"
in a community of suffering. Like Jeremiah, Christians sat
where they sat, "merging with the broad masses" and revealing secret strength in the midst of suffering. As Raymond
Fung has written,[2] "within this very ordinary reality of
daily relationships, Christians have occasions and means to
proclaim Christ." The Church today carries a stronger evangelistic impact because of its proximity to ordinary people.
The changed lives of believers on a huge scale is speaking

volumes to a spiritually hungry world. Christian witness is thus a person-to-person witness.

For example, a university professor, each Sunday after morning worship, meets students who ply him with all sorts of questions about science and the Christian faith. Another elderly professor actually had the opportunity at the end of the Cultural Revolution to explain his beliefs in person both to the late premier Zhou Enlai and to Hu Yaobang. A retired lady doctor fearlessly distributes tracts in hospital wards – even to high government officials – and gives Gospel portions to people on buses when they show an interest in what she is reading. Kinship ties often result in group conversion, and many family gatherings are experiencing almost instant growth.

Another cause of growth is the fact that God has been pleased to heal many sufferers in answer to prayer. This has been a major contributory factor in convincing the masses that there is a living God who loves and cares and with whom nothing is impossible.

Then, considering further the means that God has used to bring people to Himself, the influence of Christian radio must be given high priority. Before 1978 the response from listeners to the Far East Broadcasting Company (FEBC) and Trans-World Radio (TWR) programmes was minimal; but in 1979, following the restoration of diplomatic relations with the USA, listening to foreign stations was legalised. A flood of letters then began to pour into the offices of both agencies, testifying to the influence of their broadcasts. Before 1979 few had dared to write to the FEBC, but in 1980 TWR received nearly 7,000 letters and the following year the FEBC acknowledged 13,000 representing every province in China. These letters revealed how over the years many listeners had found new hope and a living faith in God through the programmes; people had been saved from suicide by the message of the gospel. Now a large correspondence grew up, with the number of requests for Bibles being overwhelming. One correspondent wrote: "When our brothers and sisters in Christ listen to your programmes, we really clap our hands with joy. Christians on the Mainland benefit much from them. Thousands of believers have come to the Lord recently."

Another correspondent writes:

I am a Christian of a new era. After High School I joined the People's Liberation Army . . . From 1978 to 1980 I went through a period of struggles. I was like a boat tossed in stormy seas . . . I was torn apart by my search for truth . . . I felt I did not want to live . . . It was not until the winter of 1980 when I listened to your broadcast that I gradually became released from this kind of torture. Now my spirit is receiving daily nourishment from your programmes. Thank you so much for the Bible you sent me . . . I have experienced that Christ is indeed an almighty God. The Gospel of salvation goes like a mighty wind to all corners of the world and to all corners of our homeland.

China's twenty-two provinces contain a total of 2,007 counties, and "house churches" are known to exist in almost all of them. There may be from 30,000 to 50,000 such groups altogether, representing, as they undoubtedly do, the mainstream of Christianity in China today. It is estimated that in the three years following 1980 as many as 27,000 people every day may have become Christians – something beyond the wildest dreams of missionaries thirty-five years ago. This staggering truth can only be accounted for as the result of the world-wide intercession of the fellow-members of the Body of Christ and of the fact that God's hour has come.

Harold Hinton, China "expert" and author of *Fanshen*, his once popular and enthusiastic description, written in 1950, of post-Revolution life in a Chinese village, then expressed the opinion that most Chinese Christians were "rice Christians" and that the Church was on its way to extinction. Hinton returned to China in 1980, and has since admitted that he was very badly mistaken! In spite of the dark days of trial the true Church has not only survived but flourished, emerging from virtual invisibility to be seen clearly by all. It has moved from a position of weakness to one of strength and, like the fabulous Chinese phoenix, is rising again out of the ashes of burnt Bibles and the fires of persecution. Chinese Christians are showing themselves ready to meet the challenge of taking the gospel to their own people. The corn of wheat which fell into the ground and died such a painful death is now bearing much fruit. So perhaps we may regard the nineteenth century as that of the ploughman pioneers who tilled the hard soil of China. Then, in the early twentieth century, the sowers of the good seed followed, scattering their seed in all kinds of ground. Finally, we have arrived at the time, in the 1980s, when the reaper is gathering in the ripened harvest. As one Chinese leader has said: "God is mightily at work by His Spirit as a result of the much prayer in the dark days. Now it is harvest time!" One expert in "church growth" believes that what is happening in China may be the most rapid increase in the history of Christianity. The harvest is plentiful: the yield "some a hundredfold, some sixty, some thirty".

16 The House Churches (1979–84)

"There did we rejoice in Him, who rules by His
might for ever, whose eyes keep watch on the
nations."

Psalm 66:6, 7

In the first decades of this century Roland Allen, an Anglican
missionary serving in north China, wrote books such as
Missionary Methods: St. Paul's or Ours? His revolutionary concepts of missionary work were then regarded as the vapourings of a troublesome "doctrinaire idealist". They were
only seriously considered after two world wars and a
changed world situation, and eventually recognised as
prophetic fifty years later. But long after the missionary
movement came to an end in China, the title of another
of Allen's books, *The Spontaneous Expansion of the Church*,
exactly describes what has happened in China since
1978.

Based on the smaller but stronger, well-founded and
largely clandestine cottage meetings which had courageously
maintained their existence during the Cultural Revolution,
when all structured Christianity was attacked and destroyed, there came about, as described in the previous
chapter, a mushroom growth of new believers creating an
entirely new situation. The solid core of well-grounded, tried
and tested Christians now became wellnigh swamped by
many millions of new believers, untaught and untried, whose
only background was that of Marxism and atheism. Most
of them had never seen a Bible or hymnbook and certainly

knew little of Bible history, much less of Church history or
Christian doctrine. The earlier small cottage meetings thus
grew out of all recognition into what are popularly known
as "house churches" led, in many cases, by mature Christians of an earlier period. But it must be clearly understood
that the so-called "house churches" of China can in no way
be equated with the "house church" movement in the West,
except in the sense that both seem to be the growing edge
of the Kingdom of God at the present time. Otherwise the
two differ fundamentally in their historical origins and their
general characteristics. Even in China there is no common
pattern, and the variations within this new growth of churches are considerable. But one thing the Chinese house
churches have in common is their love for Christ, for one
another and for their neighbours.

Whatever doubts there may be about the extent of the
understanding of these recent converts from atheism, there
can be no question about the authenticity of what is a
remarkable Christian movement. This new generation of
believers is fully identified with the "masses" and continues
to live within the framework of a socialist structure, seeking
to share with the people as a whole in the rebuilding of their
society through the modernisation programme. Christian
production teams have often outdone their non-Christian
counterparts in production levels and surpassed them in the
quality of their work. These Christians can certainly not be
accused of being unpatriotic: a fact which the authorities
have often acknowledged.

In the absence of formal church structures the meeting-
places of these new and large congregations vary from a
farm building or perhaps a city park to a cemetery, a fishing
boat, open fields or a secluded mountain slope. The meetings themselves are Bible-based and have a simple, non-
institutional character. Without government aid the house
churches are necessarily self-supporting, having learnt in a
hard school to make sacrifices for the maintenance of the
Lord's work. The secret of the vitality of these households
of God is found in their faithfulness and prayerfulness and

in their corporate life and patience under suffering. They constitute what is probably the most dynamic form of worship and fellowship in China today.

However, the very rapidity of the growth of these churches and the coming into being of numerous new groups lacking experienced leadership have exposed many inherent weaknesses. Few of the new believers converted since 1977 have ever had the benefit of regular Bible instruction. Seeing that not a few in the rural areas have had a limited education and have a low level of understanding of Christian truth, they tend to be experience-orientated. The lack of Bible knowledge also makes young converts susceptible to charlatans and false teachers; a number of once very zealous believers have become legalists or set themselves up as "messiahs", "angels" and advocates of strange practices.

"Witness Li" (Li Changshou), a native of Yantai and once one of Watchman Nee's inner circle of colleagues, moved to Taiwan in 1949. There he seems to have dominated the Little Flock churches while developing doctrinal emphases divergent from those of Nee's teachings. Subsequently he moved to California in the USA and promoted the "local church" movement there with its strange practices. He has also succeeded in infiltrating the former Little Flock assemblies in China – notably in Fujian, Zhejiang, Henan and Jiangxi. One practice he has advocated is that of yelling out loud when praying or of shouting at the top of one's voice the name of the Lord or verses of Scripture, to the understandable annoyance of local residents. This has earned Witness Li's followers the title of "shouters". This fanatical sect has been officially proscribed by the Chinese Government as "counter-revolutionary", and Tang Shouling, a former colleague of Li's now working with the TSPM, has collected information about the latter's activities and written a booklet about his "heresies". Unfortunately, an undiscerning public and equally undiscerning authorities often fail to distinguish between the "shouters" and normal house-church Christians, who consequently suffer through this mistaken association.

There are also frequent serious divisions on the ground of traditional church practices: the sabbath, Holy Communion, baptism, head-covering, feet-washing and so on. Other teachings in the house churches are plainly syncretistic, being a mixture of Christian concepts and concepts taken from Chinese folk religion. In view of the fact that healing has played so large a part in many conversions, the danger also exists of placing too great an emphasis on this aspect of belief.

These aberrations are confusing, not only to new believers in the house churches but also to officers of the Public Security Bureau, who find it quite impossible to distinguish between genuine religion as recognised in the Constitution and popular superstition which is denounced – a misunderstanding which frequently leads to unlawful arrest and imprisonment.

Despite these serious shortcomings and the divisions they inevitably create, visitors to the house churches usually discover a warmth of simple faith and a consuming zeal which make them feel ashamed. Clearly, however, these households of God stand in desperate need of mature Bible teachers – and in large numbers. As one old pastor expressed it: "Before the Communists came, I remember that shepherds were searching for sheep. But now, all over China, it is the sheep who are searching for shepherds!" So where are these shepherds and teachers to be found?

In 1979 the government finally decided to release cadres and intellectuals from their long detention in prison or labour camps. In Peking alone, 65,000 were released and officially rehabilitated. Among them were numerous Christian intellectuals who had been arrested in the fifties and sixties and detained ever since. They undoubtedly included large numbers of graduates of the pre-"Liberation" theological and Bible colleges. Their release certainly eased the situation, even though many of them were elderly and had been without Bibles for up to twenty-two years. Eighty-year-old Wang Mingdao was such a person, and he was released a year later, in January 1980. One ninety-year-old pastor returned to his native village in south China, and a church of 700 members grew up there in just three months! Another returned pastor in west China similarly built up a church of 400 members. These tried and tested elderly leaders had been overjoyed to discover a new generation of Christians in such large numbers and to be restored to a useful teaching ministry among them.

But God had other ways of meeting the need for leaders. Among the house churches were many young people who, though lacking in formal training, were already serving as pastors and teachers, while others were eager to be trained. For example, in 1981 sixty young people representing thirty-eight counties in Henan attended a house church training course in Kaifeng, after which eighteen were commissioned as local preachers. Others have been trained in the art of preaching, their trial sermons being tape-recorded and studied by a panel of senior pastors before the successful candidates were licensed to preach. In 1982, 400 candidates in Shandong and another 500 in Henan were waiting for training. One church leader said, "we have a five-year plan to train 1,200 full-time and lay Christian workers." Daniel, a young man who had seen his Christian father cruelly tortured to death by the Red Guards, became an earnest Christian, and his great desire was to go abroad to study for the ministry before returning to serve Christ among the churches. Half of the sixteen students of a small Bible institute in Macao come from the mainland and intend to return to witness to their own people. Meanwhile many young people are studying the Bible privately and memorising Scripture: one new convert actually memorised the entire New Testament in four months and the Psalms in only one!

Pending the formal training in China of a new generation of preachers, the radio is clearly a potential medium for providing the necessary instruction for all Christians: one person in five possesses a transistor radio, and in the big

cities possession is probably universal. Christian radio stations are broadcasting both pre-evangelism programmes
and those specially geared to the needs of Christian begin-
ners, followed by graded ones for more advanced Christians,
especially house church leaders. TWR broadcasts the *Seminary of the Air*, aimed at potential church leadership.

However, the paramount need among all the churches is
for more Bibles and for Christian literature of every kind.
When in 1966 Christians in China were largely deprived of
both, agencies in Hong Kong set about making up for these
losses, and supplies began to trickle into the Mainland. The
volume increased steadily as an average of sixty to eighty
Christians, mostly overseas Chinese, crossed the border
daily carrying two or three Bibles each for the Bible-starved
churches; other Scriptures entered China through the normal postal channels. From 1977 onwards the Chinese authorities placed no obstacles in the way of taking Bibles into
the country, so that between 1976 and 1980 a total of 500,000
to 750,000 copies were either posted or taken into the country
by travellers, eventually finding their way into the hands of
eagerly waiting Christians who were no longer afraid to be
seen in possession of them. As the number of tourists increased (seven million in 1981 alone, of whom six million
were "overseas Chinese"), so did the number of Bibles
taken into China by Christians. One organisation actually
succeeded in distributing over a million copies of the Scriptures throughout the country. Pastors who had not held a
Bible in their hands for twenty years have wept to possess
one again, while countless ordinary Christians have been
overjoyed to own one for the very first time. But these are
among the favoured ones, and millions are still waiting.
Among tens of thousands of believers in one area of Henan
Province, for example, there were fewer than thirty copies.
This dire lack in rural areas, and in some city areas too, is
quite general. By 1982 a total of one million Bibles may have
been printed within China with the authority and help of
the government. The TSPM insists that the publication and
distribution of the Bible is the sole responsibility of Chinese

Christians and that no one outside the country should carry on any activity of a missionary nature without the consent of the Chinese Church authorities. Fortunately, in spite of increasing antagonism to all imported literature, Bibles continue to find their way through every barrier to help assuage the thirst for the living Word of God. It should be added that Chinese Christians are asking not only for Bibles but also for all kinds of teaching materials, reference books and cassettes. Christian Communications Ltd of Hong Kong has prepared a set of eighteen basic works for Bible study called *The Pastor's Library* for distribution throughout China; and a collection of *Three Hundred Hymns* is also proving very popular.

For over thirty years missionaries had had no news of their Christian friends in China, though they had prayed on in faith and by name for them. Then, in 1978, with the Chinese Government giving encouragement to dollar-earning tourism, a stream of curious people from all over the world began to visit the still mysterious Middle Kingdom. In September I joined a party of young bachelor executives and some older couples on a package tour to Peking and Manchuria, ending up in Japan. It was for me a nostalgic experience, and the long rail journey back from Jilin (which, incidentally, allowed us to see a little of the devastation caused by the Tangshan earthquake of 1976) provided a unique opportunity to talk at leisure with our guide on a wide range of subjects, including religion. But the "democracy wall" and the first fraternisation between Chinese and foreigners were still several months ahead, so I was unable to make contact with any of my friends or even to have the opportunity of attending church. China was obviously struggling hard to catch up with the world. Peking, now with a population of nine million, was almost unrecognisable and not the same city as the one where I had once lived; but potentially it was a splendid functional capital, with its handsome new architecture, avenues of young trees and broad esplanades. The people were neatly dressed, and everyone looked well fed and healthy. Yet when we arrived in ultra-modern Tokyo with its fast-moving and crowded traffic and its magnificent new airport contrasting with Peking's modest, quiet terminal, it was evident that Japan was light years ahead of her giant neighbour in almost every way.

Six months later, visitors were able to make contact with mutual friends and colleagues; and when friends and former colleagues obtained my address, a wonderful correspondence followed. The joy of these reunions was unbounded, though the stories the visitors heard of suffering, suicides, deaths, denials and prison camps were harrowing in the extreme. The scars of suffering were only too apparent to the visitors, but the accounts of those who had been valiant in fight were immensely inspiring. Suffering, the visitors were told, had been the price to be paid for the purification of the Church. The Apostle Peter's rich teaching on this subject suddenly came to life and was fully illustrated in the story of the Chinese Church. A doctor writing to a friend said:

> What we have experienced from an ordinary perspective has been great suffering. However, from a spiritual perspective, what we have known has been the great blessing of being filled with God's grace . . . I know that the way to our heavenly home is the way of cross-bearing, although this is very unwelcome to the natural man. May the Lord choose people of the new creation to please Him through suffering!

And the days of suffering are certainly not at an end; indeed, the evidence was in 1983 that they were already returning. Church leaders have therefore thought it important to prepare all Christians for suffering. Thus baptismal candidates are quite normally asked the question: "Are you willing to suffer for Christ?" Said another pastor: "For Christians in China today, conversion and commitment are simultaneous: anyone who believes in God has to be prepared to sacrifice himself and to endure to the end!"

Hast thou no wound?
No wound? no scar?
Yet, as the Master shall the servant be,
And pierced are the feet that follow Me;
But thine are whole! Can he have followed far
Who has no wound, no scar?

Amy Carmichael

17   The Great Dilemma (1979–84)

"I have set my king on Zion, my holy hill . . .
Therefore, be warned, O rulers of the earth!"
                                          Psalm 2:6, 10

In 1980 the Chinese press grudgingly acknowledged that even after over thirty years of anti-religious and atheist propaganda and indoctrination there was "a mass of religious believers" in China. The change in religious policy after 1978 designed to unite the country behind the modernisation programme and the growing disillusionment with Marxism and Maoist policies had led to an unprecedented religious upsurge, especially among the country's youth, which even affected not a few Party members.

Seeing that after 1960 the TSPM had ceased to function in all but name and had faded out altogether in 1966, on its resuscitation in 1979 it had been in total abeyance for thirteen years; thus it cannot claim any credit for the remarkable increase already described. It was undoubtedly alarm within Communist Party circles at this prodigious growth of religion that led its leaders to turn again to that body which had served them so well in the fifties. Christians have never forgotten how at that time the TSPM imposed its control on the churches through the horrific accusation campaign and collaborated in the arrest and imprisonment of some of China's most outstanding leaders.

The important Party Statement on Religion published in *Red Flag* in 1982 made certain facts plainer than ever. It recognised that various religions, including Catholicism and

Protestantism, had an important place internationally and therefore went on to say: "Along with the daily increase in our international exchanges, the external contacts of the religious circles are also developing in a daily increasing manner and playing an important role in expanding our country's political influence." Thus it is plain that all TSPM delegations to North America, Europe and Australasia have had an overriding purpose, namely to extend China's political influence by presenting the church situation in China in the most favourable light possible. The Statement also says that because of its hard-won character of autonomy the Church resolutely rejects all "interference of any foreign churches" in the religious affairs of China and must never allow any foreign religious organisations to evangelise there in any way or to "smuggle large amounts of religious propaganda materials and distribute them". While there must be sympathy for the desire of Chinese Christians to preserve their autonomous status, they are surely mistaken in regarding the right hand of fellowship proffered by their Western co-believers as interference. However we look at the situation we must recognise that it is one of considerable complexity. Just as the previous chapter attempted as faithfully as possible to outline the situation relating to the house churches, this chapter now endeavours to do the same for the TSPM.

No Communist government can tolerate any challenge to its own Marxist philosophy or to its authority, and the Chinese Government will not long tolerate what it cannot control. As the Statement on Religion explicitly says: "We must strengthen the organs of government controlling religious affairs and our Party committees at all levels must powerfully *direct* and *organise* all relevant departments, including . . . the Religious Affairs Bureau." That clearly places the TSPM, despite its protests to the contrary, under the firm and direct control of the Party and explains the following events.

In January 1979 a group of Chinese ministers in Hong Kong representing several denominations paid a visit to the Mainland and were surprised to discover evidence that the

TSPM was once more in action and that church buildings long ago put to other uses were being prepared for a renewal of Christian worship. The visitors were clearly impressed, but they also discovered that the house churches, already very numerous, were deeply suspicious that this move might be a prelude to making their own meetings illegal. Those fears would soon prove to be well grounded. In July of the same year the government invited 800 leaders of the five approved religions to a meeting in Shanghai to effect the "normalisation of religious activities". The government-appointed chairman emphasised the importance of the United Front within which organisations of every kind, including the churches, could work together towards the modernisation of China.

In October 1980, after a gap of nearly twenty years, the TSPM held its Third National Conference in Nanjing: 176 delegates, including some from the "minority" peoples, approved the creation of a new body to be called the China Christian Council (CCC). The official explanation given was that the TSPM would continue to be the liaison body between the churches and the government, while the CCC, a sister organisation, would be concerned solely with a pastoral ministry in relation to all the churches of China – the two being like two arms to one body. The CCC would be neither a national Church nor a superstructure imposed upon local churches, but rather an organisation to serve all Christians and all the churches of China. The intention was clearly to win over doubters to a new organisation seemingly distinct from the old TSPM with its unsavoury reputation dating from its activities in the early fifties; but since the chairman of both bodies was Bishop Ding Guangxun and one or two of the committee members were common to both the distinction was not very convincing – and, in any case, the CCC is controlled by the TSPM. The conference frankly recognised that the majority of Christians were worshipping in numerous cottage or house meetings, and so the chairman made the following statement: "It is the duty of the TSPM to unite all the Christians in the nation. We cannot make outcasts of those Christians who worship in homes and proclaim they are illegal . . . We cannot explain the Constitution in such a way that people have the right to believe in church only and not in homes." This was a significant statement. However, while apparently giving recognition to the house churches, the TSPM let it be known that these must either accept the authority of the CCC and the TSPM or be regarded as unpatriotic. After the conference, Bishop Ding sent a cordial circular letter to all China's churches urging the fullest co-operation in the new arrangements.

Soon after this Bishop Ding, the new chairman of the TSPM (Y. T. Wu having died in 1979), in a conversation with two Hong Kong clergymen, elaborated "fourteen points" in what was called a "Call for Clarity". In this Bishop Ding praised the government for raising the people out of their poverty and increasing their morality and self-respect, and justified the emphasis on patriotism. He approved the government policy of religious freedom and, justifiably, claimed credit for the proposed modification of Article 46 of the Constitution removing the "right to promote atheism" clause. He refuted the claim that the Religious Affairs Bureau controlled the TSPM, calling the accusation a distortion. He went on to describe the function of the new body, the China Christian Council, and disowned the use of the term "official church". He refused to deny the assertion that religion had been exploited for aggression against China. He then applauded the results of applying the "three-self" principles since 1949 and called them irreversible. Bishop Ding further claimed that the Church in China was more united than ever before, and that there was no division between the "three-self churches" and the "house churches". Insisting that the Chinese Church itself should assume sole responsibility for evangelistic work in that country, he urged that there must be no reversion to the days of "foreign missions" or "denominations". While Bishop Ding expressed a wish for helpful international contacts, he differentiated between "friendly" groups who supported the TSPM and "enemies" who did not. The latter, he alleged, were people who, while promoting prayer for China and undertaking "research", were actually collecting intelligence and engaging in "hate China" propaganda.

The "fourteen points" certainly clarified Bishop Ding's position. With some points no one would want to disagree; but others are clearly open to question as to their factual nature, while the final accusations are themselves gross distortions and totally untrue. Bishop Ding leaves no room for doubt about his antagonism towards evangelicals abroad and his alignment with his uncritical ecumenical friends. Seeing that most of the well-informed Christians in China look to the evangelicals of the world for their prayer support and sympathy, they will not appreciate Dr Ding's attitude.

The first positive action to be taken by the revived TSPM was the recovery and reopening of church buildings for Christian worship: first in Shanghai, and then in a growing number of other cities. It is probable that the Communist Party, when it modified its policy on ethnic minorities and religious believers in 1978, was deceived by its own propaganda, expecting that "only a few old folk would come tottering out of the shadows to attend a few reopened churches". Its members must have been surprised and shocked by what actually happened. On September 2nd 1979, the former Moore Memorial Church in Shanghai held a thanksgiving service which was attended by 2,000 people, many of whom were queuing at 6 a.m. to ensure a seat! One hesitant worshipper described her experience in these words:

> So I went to church. It was heavenly. My heart was full of blessings and my eyes full of happy tears. I shamelessly clutched the arm of an old man sitting next to me, wetting his jacket with my tears. I was so happy I had a headache. My heart beat fast every time the congregation sang and the piano played. It was too much for me. Now I can only remember the sermon title. It was "Jesus is my Shepherd".

Three Sunday services were subsequently arranged to accommodate the crowds, and a second church was reopened;

church buildings in Ningbo, Fuzhou, Amoy, Suzhou and Canton were also reopened at the same time. The numbers that flocked to attend were in some places so huge that admission tickets had to be issued. Tourists fortunate enough to attend were amazed at what they found and received a joyous welcome from the worshippers.

The second achievement of the TSPM was the gaining of government permission for the printing of over one million copies of the complete Bible or New Testament. They were to be printed on paper supplied by the government and on the presses of the Commercial Press in Shanghai. Interestingly enough, the new simplified script would not be used, and the 1919 Union Version was their choice. More interestingly still, the term used for "God" would not be *Shangti* (Supreme Ruler), as traditionally used by most denominational churches, but *Shen* (Spirit), as favoured by most indigenous groups and by evangelicals in general. Once the Bibles were in print the TSPM claimed that it was providing sufficient copies to meet the need and that therefore it was quite unnecessary for Christians any longer to ask for or receive Bibles from abroad. If, as the TSPM recently claimed, there were only three million Christians in China, this argument might have had some validity; but in fact that estimate is today manifestly unrealistic and the shortage of Bibles, especially among the rural churches, remains acute. In one county in central China, for instance, among 90,000 Christians there were only twenty-six Bibles, while in one city in Gansu Province, tens of thousands of believers had only thirty between them; in Shaanxi Province fifty New Testaments had to meet the need of 6,000 Christians. The hunger for the Scriptures among the many millions of Christians in the house churches remains intense, and one such group sent its representatives on an 850-mile journey in search of Bibles. Fujian Province alone ordered 20,000 copies; and in an area between Shanghai and Hangzhou where a huge "people's movement" has arisen 100,000 were ordered to meet its needs. So Hong Kong continues to answer the plea for Bibles, cassettes and Christian literature using every possible legitimate means to do so, in spite of the stricter controls imposed. In the Amoy Customs House a large sign appeared in 1983 warning travellers that the Bible and other kinds of Christian literature were prohibited items for import. More recently, Christian university students in Peking have been ordered to hand in all Bibles and literature received from abroad or risk dismissal. It must be clear that the government cannot allow unlimited Bible distribution, which might make the Bible the most visible book in towns and villages; nevertheless, in addition to the bibles printed by the TSPM a number of churches are printing quantities of them and hymnbooks locally to meet their own needs.

Within China, however, the authorities have rehabilitated the Bible and removed the ban on reading it, declaring it to be an outstanding work of literature. A lecture on the Bible and Christianity given in 1980 at Nanjing University attracted an overflow audience of students. It is also interesting to note that, under the Chinese Academy of Social Sciences in Peking, the government has set up an Institute for the Study of World Religions, though such studies are naturally from a Marxist point of view. However, in 1982 the Institute invited Hans Küng, the German theologian, to lecture on "the existence of God"!

Besides securing the reopening of many churches for worship and the printing of Bibles, the CCC has also recognised the need to train future clergy for the churches. It was already aware of the way in which the house churches at grass-roots level had been training young people in quite large numbers for their own work. In 1980, therefore, it reopened the theological seminary in Nanjing, the first class numbering forty-seven, including some women. The new students were so ignorant of Bible content that the first year was given almost entirely to familiarising them with the Scriptures. At the same time, the CCC issued a magazine or study syllabus – not strictly a correspondence course – containing study guides designed to help house church leaders. This magazine was edited by a former Pentecostal pastor and originally had a circulation of about 40,000. Subsequently, a number of junior colleges have been opened in Peking, Fujian and Sichuan to feed the seminary in Nanjing, which will soon have a capacity for 200 students. Additional junior colleges are planned for Shanghai, Hangzhou, Chengdu and Wuhan. Other city centres have held short courses of training for village lay leaders. "Political awareness" is one of the conditions of entry into these colleges, and some applicants have been rejected for lack of such a qualification. Students are encouraged to study Marxism–Leninism, though this subject is not actually on the curriculum. Music and the arts are also developed, and fellowship, testimony and prayer meetings fill the evenings.

Under the auspices of the CCC, churches all over China steadily reopened at the rate of about one a week until now, in 1984, more than 1,600 churches are in use for Protestant worship, most of which have been redecorated by the government with funds provided in lieu of rent for their past use. A team of from three to six pastors, mostly elderly and trained in the thirties and forties, normally serves each church. They represent different denominations and so present the image of a "post-denominational" Church. Almost certainly, one or more members of each team have a political function; but, for the first time, the pastors have been told that they may preach from the Bible in whatever way they wish. For example, at the first service for twenty-two years held in Chongqing, the minister preached on the Second Coming of Christ and the need for the new birth, both topics previously under a ban.

No one questions the fact that although the top TSPM leaders are mostly theologians of the liberal school the majority of the clergy serving in the open churches have theologically conservative backgrounds. And because the majority of the worshippers are evangelical Christians, pastors who preach Biblical sermons draw the largest congregations. Some sermons, however, are little more than thinly disguised Communist propaganda designed to keep Christians aware of the political line. It is also common knowledge that not a few of these "political" pastors openly denied the faith during the Cultural Revolution and took an active part in the persecution of Christians. In the eyes of many true Christians, therefore, they deserve to be labelled "apostates" or "Judases". Their re-employment by the CCC has been a major reason for the widespread distrust of the TSPM and the CCC among the house churches. So inevitably there are tensions surrounding the work of both bodies. Turning again to the Statement on Religion, the paragraph relating to "religious workers" says: "We must satisfactorily arrange the lives of professional workers ... especially the well-known personalities and intellectuals among them and grant them proper remuneration." The clergy are thus in the pay of the government, the top TSPM leaders being very well paid. Even the average salary is 100Y a month, which is much higher than the average wage in China.

Wherever the TSPM reopened churches, huge and enthusiastic crowds flocked to attend. By Easter 1983 between 20,000 and 30,000 worshippers were attending fifteen reopened churches in Shanghai alone. In Hangzhou, capital of Zhejiang Province, 20,000 people were attending seventeen services in five churches and 400 the mid-week Bible study; and in two years over 600 had been baptised. The former Griffith John Memorial Church in Hankou was beautifully redecorated for its reopening in 1982, the congregation numbering, by contrast, from 300 to 400 with seventy or so attending a midweek fellowship meeting. But it must be remembered that in the Wuhan area ultra-left sympathies still prevail and there is much anti-religious feeling. In Canton three churches have been reopened, in one of which 2,000 attended the first Communion service; while in the small city where Dr Sun Yat-sen was born 1,000 people celebrated Christmas in the newly opened church. In Xian, famous for its 300 BC terracotta warriors, 30,000 Christians have registered their names with the CCC. Yet these large weekly congregations in the reopened churches represent only a small fraction of the total number of Christians in China today.

The majority of Christians are to be found in the house churches, which did not entirely share the euphoria about the relaxed religious policy. The government's attitude was ambivalent and pragmatic, its policy being freedom but freedom within bounds. Among the clauses in the section relative to religion in the fourth revised Constitution (1982) there occurs the significant phrase: "The state protects *legitimate* religious activities", clearly meaning activities approved by the RAB and the TSPM, all others being judged illegitimate or illegal. So the noose had been drawn tighter and freedom diminished even further. The government-controlled press continued to attack religion but often failed to distinguish between those religions recognised in the 1982 Statement and mere superstition, of which there had also been a widespread revival in the forms of idolatry, witchcraft, fortune-telling, spiritualism and Taoist occult activity. That Statement said: "We should clearly differentiate between normal religious activities and illegal criminal activities." Nevertheless the door was left open for either the TSPM or the local police agencies to accuse the house churches of illegitimate activities, and they were soon to do so.

Herein lies the dilemma. Obviously, large numbers of Christians have decided that in spite of serious misgivings, they must support the CCC and the officially recognised churches. A majority, in view of the record of TSPM oppression in the fifties and of the fact that it is the creation of the Communist Party and therefore ultimately under the control of an atheist government dedicated to the elimination of religion, will for reasons of conscience have nothing to do with that organisation, comparing it to the tares sown among the wheat or the thorns and thistles which choke the growth of the seed and threaten the harvest. Having come to prefer the more informal style of the house churches, they insist on their constitutional freedom to continue worshipping in their own homes or privately. There are also those who, for various reasons, remain aloof from both CCC churches and the house churches. These would include the secret Christians who hold important positions in government, in the universities or in medicine, and many intellectuals.

This leaves as a burning issue the question of who has the right to speak for the Church in China. TSPM delegates who have visited the USA, Canada, Europe and Australasia have claimed to be the sole spokesmen of an undivided Church; but such a claim cannot possibly be substantiated, because very large numbers of Christians simply do not recognise the CCC as having that right. On the other hand, these non-conformers, while refusing to acknowledge the CCC as their spokesman and having as yet no co-ordinating organisation of their own, do not themselves speak with one voice. In view of the diversity of tradition and of theological convictions it is likely to be a long time before the house churches achieve any degree of unanimity.

In spite of some of their public statements, both the CCC and the TSPM are clearly opposed to any house church movement which remains outside their own control. In proportion as the number of reopened churches has increased, the insistence by the CCC that where there is an open church building the house churches should close has become steadily stronger; and this in spite of the fact that the house churches gained legal status in 1980. The *Red Flag* article stated: "Christians meeting in homes should, in principle, not be permitted, but they should not be rigidly prohibited." In a Marxist society, however, no sector can expect to be free from government control, and at the Shanghai Conference of 1981 one of the speakers put the matter bluntly: "To be anti-TSPM is to be anti-government, for religion must be organised and under control." The truth of this is obvious, and we should recognise that it is quite impossible to apply Western criteria of freedom to China.

The Chinese Government, being security-conscious and therefore suspicious of all secret gatherings, fears that house churches not under its control could be subversive. The TSPM, therefore, having pledged its prior loyalty to the Communist Party, is a prisoner of the system and so has no option but to carry out the policies of that Party and to try to compel house churches to accept its authority. Since 1982 all these churches have been kept under close surveillance. The CCC in several provinces has issued a list of prohibitions which includes such items as teaching religion to those under eighteen, holding meetings outside designated buildings and led by undesignated preachers and travelling outside designated areas to spread religion (the "three designates"). Another prohibition says: "Do not pray every day, only on Sundays!" – hopefully meaning merely no weekday meetings! Edicts like these have only served to increase the tension between the open churches and the house churches.

The TSPM has in numerous instances been known to call in the Public Security Bureau to help it enforce the closure of churches or bring them under control. In 1982 reports of open clashes and violence in two places in Zhejiang Province between local churches and the Public Security Bureau featured in the world's press. Since then matters have become increasingly serious. In November of that year churches in Henan were ordered to suspend all meetings and Christians were forbidden to listen to foreign radio stations. Some of the leaders were severely beaten, an incident which brings back memories of the Cultural Revolution. In Shanghai, 200 house churches were forced by the TSPM to disband and warned not to listen to Christian radio programmes which were alleged to be hostile to China. In Shandong Province one church leader died when a house meeting was stormed, and other leaders were arrested, bound and made to kneel in prison for three days and nights. As 1983 progressed things became progressively worse and the CCC increasingly intolerant, ordering the closure of all house churches in the major cities. Some house churches were ordered to combine to form one congregation under CCC control, and that body even insisted on its right to transfer local leaders from one church to another; in fact, anyone outside the approved organisations engaging in religious activities becomes by definition a criminal or a "reactionary element", and all house church activities are implicitly illegitimate. In 1984 most house churches were enduring heavy pressure to conform. But if all the old church buildings in China were to be reopened they would be totally insufficient to hold the millions of new believers. So the TSPM is prepared to give recognition to "meeting points" or house churches which accept its authority. More than 10,000 have done so. However, the TSPM does not intend to reopen all churches and is pledged only to restore the situation as it was before 1966. During 1984 the number of arrests has continued to increase. In Henan alone, 110 house church pastors were in detention or prison, some serving three- to five-year sentences, while arrest warrants had been issued for 130 itinerant evangelists. Members of Witness Li's proscribed "shouting" sect have been arrested as "counter revolutionaries", and the campaign has been used to attack a wider circle of house churches where praying in unison has long been practised.

As the TSPM has set up more and more regional local committees, so its ability to control and restrict the activities of house churches has become greater. There have been many cases of persecution – with meetings disrupted and their participants beaten and gaoled as the result of the zeal of local TSPM officials collaborating with the police. At least thirteen provinces have reported many such incidents of repression. TSPM officials also collaborate with the police in monitoring and reporting unofficial activities, sending informers into house meetings and assisting with interrogation.

In England, Christians once burnt their fellow Christians at the stake, and a similar tragedy could easily be re-enacted in China. One can only hope and pray that the government and the TSPM will learn the lesson of history, and of recent years in China, that the greater the persecution, the faster the growth of the Church: Pharaoh discovered to his dismay that "the more the Israelites were oppressed, the more they multiplied abroad" (Exodus 1:12).

Indeed, the modes of survival and propagation which house churches have devised through experience over the past twenty years will stand them in good stead. Sometimes, for example, a large house church ordered to close will break up into a number of smaller groups and thus multiply itself.

And once again, it is the young women who are stepping into the shoes of the arrested pastors and evangelists and sacrificially carrying on a pastoral ministry.

So what of "religious freedom" in China today? Marxists believe that, under their scientific system and with proper education, religion will ultimately wither away. In September 1982, the chief of the RAB was addressing a meeting of TSPM and CCC leaders when, with unusual frankness, he said: "To respect and protect freedom of religious belief has always been China's attitude to religion and the government is determined to enforce this policy until religion dies out naturally!" Therefore, while paying lip-service in the Constitution to freedom of religious belief, the policy of all Communist parties the world over has been to hasten the demise of religion by all possible means. Their tactics are always pragmatic. Russia showed tolerance of religious believers during the Second World War when the Church gave that country its full support against Nazi Germany; but then, under Khrushchev, thousands of churches were closed and Christians persecuted for their faith. In China the Christian Church suffered terribly during the Cultural Revolution; but when the government wanted to enlist its co-operation in the "Four Modernisations" programme, the pressure was relaxed.

Each of the four Constitutions so far has included the item "freedom of religious belief", but the 1978 text shows some development from the earlier texts, promising as it does no compulsion to believe or not to believe and no discrimination against believers. But the phrase "the state protects *legitimate* religious activities" raises the question of what is included in the word "legitimate". In any case, as a senior pastor in Shanghai once remarked, "Policy is one thing, its implementation is another." The freedom that Chinese Christians may enjoy will always be carefully guided by Communist ideology, and will be determined by the stability of the government and not by what the Constitution says. Everyone in China is wondering what will happen when Deng Xiaoping dies.

One observer of religion in the Communist world describes the process like this: first, freedom is limited; then sanctions are imposed; next, an enforced unity among all kinds of church leaders is sought; then other liberties are removed one by one; and, finally, new leaders are appointed upon whom more restrictions are imposed. In this way the Church is gradually muzzled by deterrents and intimidation.

Chinese Christians have long learnt to live with fear and to face both external pressures (such as job discrimination, the deprivation of higher education opportunities for their children and the inability to find suitable marriage partners) and internal pressures deriving from lack of fellowship and a solid Christian foundation. Such pressures can easily lead to compromises of all kinds, and it is true that many have weakened under these and more sinister ones.

During 1983 events on the political scene soon affected the churches and the house churches in particular. The Party, in which Deng Xiaoping still held the power, had three major concerns: the determination to purge itself of the ultra-left Mao sympathisers, the rising crime rate and the threat from the penetration of Western "bourgeois" influences.

To deal with the problem of crime – robberies, rapes and murders – targets were set for the number of arrests and executions in every city. By November 1983 as many as 5,000 executions had taken place, many of them in public. However much this draconian method may conflict with human rights, it seems to have had a salutary effect, and crime has diminished. Not all criminals have been so fortunate as those depicted in a Harbin gaol in *The Heart of the Dragon*, a series of documentaries shown on British TV early in 1984. Unfortunately, many Christians were arrested in the wake of the anti-crime drive and accused of "illegal activities".

The planned three-year anti-leftist purge of the forty-million-strong Communist Party ("Party rectification") decided on at the Sixth National People's Congress was designed to weed out large numbers of half-educated, incompetent time-servers loyal to Mao who had been admitted to the Party during the Cultural Revolution and who, in many cases, were resisting Deng Xiaoping's policies. But this anti-left drive was overtaken by an anti-right or anti-intellectual crusade against what was called "spiritual pollution". This included all foreign "bourgeois" influences flooding into China with the modernisation programme: youth clothing styles, women's make-up and hair-styles, disco dancing and pop music, videotapes and pornography. Authors writing about "sex and religion" were accused of posing an ideological threat. Yet even more threatening to China's ideology was the spread among intellectuals and youth of Western liberal, existential and cultural ideas or "creeping capitalism". The threatened leftists still in positions of influence therefore seized the opportunity to shift the spotlight from themselves on to the rightists and "bourgeois liberals". But the attempt failed, and in 1984 the anti-pollution campaign was fading fast; other than pushing their own Marxist concepts about morality and discussion about "socialist spiritual civilisation", China's leaders were plainly perplexed as to how to combat "spiritual pollution". They felt that socialism itself was under threat; not surprisingly, therefore, all cassette tapes, books and literature from abroad were suspect, including all religious material. Consequently, anyone known to be receiving either Bibles or other literature from abroad or from tourists was likely to be in trouble. The local Public security bureaux were searching out offenders. And tourists found that every attempt was made to keep them isolated from personal contacts – and even to keep them segregated in church!

In these several campaigns it has been all too easy for the authorities to level charges of law-breaking against the house-church leaders, many of whom were forced to undergo correctional training under the tutelage of the RAB and the TSPM.

From what has been detailed in this chapter it is clear that the TSPM has a number of considerable achievements to its credit: the opening of many churches, the printing of

Bibles and the reopening of theological colleges. But it is equally clear that it always acts as an instrument of government religious policy. The phenomenal growth of the house churches has created a dilemma for the TSPM too: it finds itself once again in the probably unwelcome role of the oppressor. Its credibility is at stake.

The Church in China has certainly achieved independence from foreign control and financial support – but is the TSPM really true to its name? Being controlled by the government, the open churches are scarcely "self-governing". Since the State pays the salaries of the preachers and officials, and provides other subsidies, neither are the churches "self-supporting". And the claim to be "self-propagating" needs further examination. The TSPM leaders define that term as a refusal to allow any outside agency to share in the responsibility for the evangelisation of China as this would undo the achievement of the past thirty years. They are antagonistic towards anyone who wishes to support the Chinese Church in its huge task, regarding evangelicals in particular, on these grounds, as being hostile to China. The TSPM rejects as interference in China's affairs all forms of international co-operation or mutual aid, although both are implicit in the concept of the Body of Christ. By reason of its "selfhood" the TSPM even protests against the broadcasts by foreign Christian radio stations, whose programmes have brought hope and joy to so many millions of listeners. So, if all outside assistance and co-operation is to be refused, does the TSPM itself accept responsibility for the enormous task of evangelising a quarter of the human race within its own country?

While in London in 1982 Bishop Ding seemed to downgrade the concept of evangelism, placing it second in importance to working for the modernisation of China. Nor does he appear to accept the Great Commission of Matthew 28 as imperative, emphasising rather the priority of the "Christian presence" in Chinese society. Even Miss Jiang Peifen, a CCC committee member who has described herself as an "evangelical", said in Montreal in 1981 that she no longer drew a sharp distinction between believers and unbelievers; nor did she regard non-believers as "children of hell", but saw "Jew and Gentile as both lambs of the Lord and equally objects of His redemption" – the familiar universalist position, but certainly not that of evangelical theologians. The "Ten Prohibitions" issued by several provincial TSPM authorities are categorical: "Keep religion to yourself and do not travel from commune to commune to spread religion!" All this would seem to suggest that, in the minds of the TSPM leaders, "no propagation" has replaced the original imperative of "self-propagation"!

The foregoing assessment is certainly not the picture of the TSPM that its members themselves would wish to project to the world. It is rather a picture of an organisation which, in spite of every protest to the contrary, is securely under the control of a government pledged to eliminate religion and to promote atheism. It exists to carry out the religious policies of the government and functions within clear guide-lines established by the ruling Communist Party. The TSPM leaders may well be acting in a way which they believe to be in the best interests of the Christians and of the churches in China under the circumstances. But in the light of the facts recorded in this chapter – and they are facts, not accusations – the sole conclusion possible is that they are mistaken and misguided. How wonderful it would be if they too were to experience the spirit of revival, if their eyes could be opened to see the issues clearly and if their hearts could be filled with love for their brothers and sisters in Christ whom they are now persecuting and seeking to dominate! A coming together of the true members of the Body of Christ at present found in both the open and in the house churches would surely bring glory to God and hasten the evangelisation of China's one billion people.

Dr J. H. Taylor III of the Overseas Missionary Fellowship has written: "As Christians, our response should express consideration that seeks to grasp the complexity and sensitivity of the situation, confidence that sees our sovereign Lord working out His purposes, and concern that issues from love in prayer and prudent action."

18   God's Highway (1983——)

"Behold the Lord comes with might, and His arm
rules for Him."

Isaiah 40:10

There is no doubt that the days of the Acts of the Apostles
are today being repeated in many parts of the world. In the
face of fierce persecution the churches of Russia, Mozam-
bique, little Laos and mighty China – all under the iron
rule of Communist governments – are displaying amazing
boldness in their witness. The number of believers is being
greatly multiplied, and there is abundant, convincing evidence of God's miracle-working power. In parts of China
the Spirit of revival is sweeping through the churches once
again. As Isaiah prophesied: "When the enemy shall come
in like a flood, the Spirit of the Lord shall lift up a standard
against him." (Isaiah 59:19, AV)

But what of the future? Can this religious revival
continue unchallenged by its Marxist enemies? How
will possible political changes affect the Church? The
Church may be larger than ever, but can it overcome
its inherent weaknesses to become a powerful influence
for God in a socialist society? Or does it contain the
seeds of decline in the face of satanic opposition? And
are there really no ways in which Christian aid can
reach China without causing unnecessary offence?

Taking up the last question first: most Christian leaders
in the West would now accept that any reversion to the old
patterns of missionary work in China is not only undesirable

but also impossible. Any attempt at independent action on the part of foreign missionary organisations would not only be rejected by the Chinese Government but would be offensive to Chinese Christians who, while appreciating the contribution that missionaries made in the past, are now proud of their hard-won autonomous status. But that fact does not rule out for ever the possibility – given goodwill on both sides – of various forms of Christian aid to China now and, hopefully, of genuine co-operation in the future among the members of the Body of Christ inside and outside that vast nation. The latter could include co-operation in theological training, in the supply of Bibles and Christian literature and in the important sphere of radio broadcasting.

But there already exist varieties of opportunity for Christians to make their contribution to China's modernisation. For instance, one Christian organisation sent a few English teachers to a certain university. The authorities, knowing that they were Christians, watched them with a wary eye and warned the students against being "corrupted" by their ideas. But after a year had passed, the same authorities were so impressed by the excellence of their teaching and by their exemplary lives that they requested many more teachers for the following year. Now the requests for their teachers far outnumber the teachers available. Among the many hundreds of foreign teachers working in China there are well over 100 committed Christians. They are not missionaries in disguise, as the TSPM alleges, but are seeking to make a Christian contribution to the education of China's youth. Many more Christians are serving as scientists and engineers; and their opposite numbers, taught to believe that all religion is unscientific superstition, are surprised and intrigued to find that scientists can also be Christians. The future scope for such "tent-makers" seems to be unlimited, given the right approach and wise management.

Another significant venture is the Jian Hua ("Building up China") Foundation, a non-profit welfare organisation founded by Christian overseas Chinese dedicated to helping China in her modernisation programme. Jian Hua is assist-

ing China with a US thirty-million dollar China International Cultural Exchange Centre in Peking. Besides the cultural
centre, the Foundation will arrange and finance a scholarly
exchange programme and also channel emergency relief
when natural disasters strike. Needless to say, this project
has had the welcome and full support of the Chinese government from the start. China, therefore, is not averse to
accepting aid from Christian agencies that respect her
sovereignty and do not infringe the Church's independence.

The fact that God is in control of human history and
destiny is well illustrated by the story of Cyrus, the pagan
king whom God called His "shepherd" and His "anointed".
The way Cyrus ordered the release of Israel from captivity
and arranged for her return to her own land is an outstanding
example of God's sovereign control over men and nations
and has a direct bearing on the situation in China.

As already detailed in my book *New Spring in China*[1], the
same obstacles which once hindered the spread of the gospel
in China also hindered the Communists in their mission to
the Chinese people: namely the lack of a single national
language spoken and understood by all of that country's
major races and regions; widespread illiteracy, especially in
the rural areas; Confucian culture, regarded by the Communists as feudalistic and conservative and by Christians as a
major hindrance on account of the hold that ancestor
worship had on all Chinese; the vice-like grip of Buddhism,
Taoism and a variety of folk and animistic superstitions in
which the people were held; and finally the crippling lack
of adequate communications which, well into the twentieth
century, reduced travel to crawling carts, mules, camels,
river boats and foot-slogging. Missionaries were in no position to do anything about any of these hindrances to their
work, but the Communist government has successfully
popularised the Peking dialect as the "common language"
of all the people of China, greatly reduced illiteracy, under-
mined the hold of Confucian ideas on personal conduct and
social life, campaigned against superstitious religion and
made great strides in creating a network of roads, railways

and air services. Isaiah (Ch. 40) prophesied the early return
of Israel to Jerusalem: all natural barriers would be overcome, a highway for God would appear and the glory of the
Lord would be revealed. He went on to exalt the Lord God
in all His majesty as sovereign in creation and in history,
whose Word abides when works like the *Little Red Book* are
forgotten and who humbles proud rulers like the Gang of
Four and regards proud nations as nothing and emptiness.

So the God who in His sovereign power and wisdom used
Cyrus to do His will is now using those who deny His
existence to fulfil His eternal purposes for China. The early
Church praised God that the very people united in their
opposition to the progress of the Gospel – Herod, Pilate,
the Gentiles, Israel – instead of stopping the work of God
only succeeded in doing whatever God's hand and God's
plan had predetermined should take place (Acts 4:27, 28).
So today there is "a highway for our God" in China; there
is also a purified and enlarged Church. Now the world waits
to see the glory of the Lord revealed!

How prepared are China's Christians to march forward
along God's royal highway? We in the West feel humbled
as we read the story of the sufferings of the Chinese Church.
We have much to learn from her experience: her devotion
to the Word of God, her confidence in the power of prayer,
her patience under suffering, her loyalty to Christ at any
cost, her refusal to compromise and her costly obedience to
evangelism. But sadly it must be said that, like Israel returning from exile, the Church in China has yet to put her house
in order and is facing a Herculean task of reconstruction
and reorganisation. At the risk of seeming presumptuous
and of offering gratuitous advice, I can list at least eight
spheres in which a Spirit-filled leadership needs to think
deeply and Biblically and so show the way ahead.

Heading the list must be the search for unity, the need
for which featured so largely in Our Lord's prayer as He
faced crucifixion. The strength of a Church under an
alien tyranny must be her unity: not the superficial
organisational unity which some claim now exists but the

true spiritual unity which exists only within the Body of Christ, the born-again community of true believers found both in the house churches and in the CCC churches. Her present fragmentation can only keep the Church in a position of weakness and, as in the case of the Jews rebuilding Jerusalem, make her highly vulnerable to enemy attack. Here the way ahead is full of pitfalls and problems, but the goal must be kept clearly in sight. And Christians outside China must do nothing to deepen the divisions but should rather pray earnestly for the unity for which Our Lord prayed.

Next, surely, must be the old issue of the Church's cultural identity. The Chinese have always had a great pride in their ethical culture and unique world-view, which is something that missionaries rarely succeeded in coming to grips with. Christianity was always seen as an exotic transplant, and missionaries in general failed to find ways to reach the heart of China in order to perfect and transform that country's life and thought. The task of making the Church truly Chinese must be a major concern. And this goes far deeper than applying "three-self" principles.

Then, following on the matter of cultural identity, is the large and vexed question of indigenous church structures. Visitors in recent years, refreshed by the increasing informality and spontaneity of much worship in the West, have been disappointed to find the open churches still running in the old ruts of formal services, carbon copies of traditional Western church worship: even in a so-called "post-denominational" era, "bishops" still proudly wear their distinctive Western style clerical dress and vestments! Church leaders and theologians will have to wrestle with a number of practical and theological questions relating to the ministry and the laity, the forms of sacraments and ways of public worship. The TSPM wants to reject Western models, but as yet has discovered no alternative. Should theology be restated in Chinese terms, and with the background of Chinese thought and culture in view?

Then, sooner or later, the Church must reach an

understanding of the essential differences between a Biblical and a Marxist world-view and be able to defend religion against those who, like Marxists, dismiss it as unscientific. The Church must consider how the Christian faith can best be preserved and strengthened under an atheist government. If the Christian Church, as St. Peter urges, is to "make a defence" to Marxists "when called on to account for the hope that is in them", then it needs to strengthen its intellectual understanding of its own faith and demonstrate that Christianity offers a more radical and powerful solution to society's problems.

Closely related to the foregoing is the problem of how to present Christian doctrine in a Chinese context. It was unfortunate that the early translators used the Buddhist word for "suffering" to mean "sin" and so caused confusion. Confucian thought had little place for sin, and certainly Marxism dismisses the topic, believing that all that is wrong with the world lies in a wrong ordering of society, not in the heart of man. But it is here that the Christian view of sin as selfishness should be well understood by all Chinese, whose Maoist slogan was "Fight self, serve others!", even though they would not at first understand sin as rebellion against God and His laws. The truth of reconciliation with God and with man is another topic which can suggest an answer to the Maoist's problem of alienation and "contradiction".

Taking the concept of sin as selfishness, the Christian should be able to demonstrate that man being what he is by nature – a fallen being – the Communist vision of the totally selfless "new man" is unattainable. As the Communist folk idol Che Guevara once said: "If our revolution does not have the goal of changing men, it doesn't interest me!" The theory that by changing men the structure of society can be changed is nowhere evidenced in the history of revolution. But Christianity does have a life-changing power, and a power which has changed society and nations. And if the ideal of selfless service can be found anywhere, surely it is in the person

of Jesus Christ, who said "I am among you as He that
serveth!"

This provides the cue for a Christian life-style in a
socialist society. In China, it is impossible for the individual
or the church to opt out of a collective system in which
the "unit" (*danwei*) totally controls the lives of individuals.
Joseph Ton of Romania once wrote in an article:

> We Christians have a place in a socialist society . . .
> We have not chosen Christ but He has chosen us.
> Since, therefore, He chose us from within socialism, it
> means He wants us here . . . The divine task of the
> evangelical Christian living in a socialist society is to
> lead such a correct and beautiful life that he will
> demonstrate to that society that he and he alone is the
> "new man" that socialism seeks vainly to create. This
> will be the really convincing evidence of the truth of
> Christianity.

Finally, Chinese Christians must reach conclusions
about the Biblical view of Church-State relations and the
contemporary application of Our Lord's words "Render
unto Caesar the things that are Caesar's and to God the
things that are God's." This has never been an easy
matter, but it is obviously vital. Unless the churches can
find answers to these problems they will be in danger of
degenerating into a pietistic and socially irrelevant minority. If the Cultural Revolution generation now claim to
be the leaders of thought in China, then Christians too
need to be thinking and praying a great deal about their
future in Chinese society.

All these problems confronting the Chinese Church
should guide the prayers of Christians world-wide in the
months and years to come. The closing sentence of *Come
Wind, Come Weather (1960)*[2] reads: "The present dusk is not
the dusk of day's end, but the dusk that precedes the dawn!"
Although the dark night of the Cultural Revolution terror
followed, the dawn of that new day for the Church has now

come. Greatly strengthened and not weakened by persecution, the revived churches are boldly embarking, in obedience to the risen Lord's command, on the task of evangelising their own people. The negative attitudes of the TSPM towards evangelism have had no appeal for Christians who have experienced the transforming power of Christ and are impelled by His constraining love to make Him known. They realise that the majority of their one billion fellow citizens have never heard the Good News of Christ's saving work on the Cross, and they firmly believe that God has entrusted Chinese Christians with the monumental task of evangelising their own people. They are determined to be genuinely "self-propagating" and, undismayed by the prohibitions and threats of the TSPM, are travelling from village to village, from county to county and from province to province at great personal cost, to spread the gospel message. They are taking the offensive against the enemy.

Among many examples there is one of the old pastor who travelled throughout Anhui and Jiangxi Provinces preaching to hundreds in the open fields. When he was arrested and cruelly beaten, even the non-Christians protested vehemently to the local authorities. A letter from Henan Province written in 1982 tells a similar story. Ten young men and women, after earnest prayer, set out to preach, and as they proclaimed the gospel with tears, passers-by stopped to listen, fortune-tellers broke down and wept, and workers on their way home from the factories forgot their hunger and stayed to listen as God's power was present. The large crowd would not let them stop, tired though they were. But then the Public Security Bureau officials arrived, tied up the young preachers and dragged them away to be beaten unconscious. When one girl of only fourteen, after being thus beaten, revived and continued witnessing, all kinds of people broke down, repented and believed in Jesus. Four of the young men were arrested and forced to kneel for three days without food or water, but even as they were being beaten until the blood flowed they continued praying, singing and praising the Lord until even their tormentors were convicted and believed the gospel. "So, in this area", said the writer, "recently the flame of the Gospel has spread everywhere. There has never been a revival here before, but through persecution this place has truly received the seeds of life."

In 1982 churches in Zhejiang and Henan Provinces actually commissioned their own missionaries – as many as ninety from one county alone – to go to far distant provinces to preach the gospel. They travelled as far as Sichuan in the west, Yunnan and Guizhou in the south-west and Guangxi in the south. One Christian went on a vacation to Tibet, where he led thirty-seven people to Christ, including ten Tibetans.

The CCC was quick to condemn all such activities, and renewed its orders forbidding preachers to go outside their own areas. The RAB in Xian complained that the growth of one church in the city to over 3,000 was due to itinerant preachers, one of whom had "converted" 800 of his work unit of 12,000! All itinerant evangelists have become targets for arrest, and one such was suspended by his thumbs and beaten. Some of these evangelists, knowing that warrants for their arrest had been issued, have feared to return home and so continue preaching in exile while their Christian brethren look after their families who sometimes face real poverty.

In 1983 house-church leaders in central China met to discuss how to continue evangelistic work in face of the TSPM restrictions on such activity, and a courageous joint guide-line for work under these conditions was adopted. Christians do not intend to be intimidated or deflected from making Christ known throughout China. One letter written to the FEBC expresses perfectly what, in face of growing opposition, most Christians believe: "Brothers, do not worry about us. Our heavenly Father cares for us. Everywhere there is Christ's grace and with the Holy Spirit in our midst preserving us and with the addition of your prayers on our behalf, we deeply believe that the day when the Gospel will go all over China is fast approaching!"

As long ago as the seventeenth century, Samuel Ruther-
ford wrote: "Faith is better for the free air and the sharp
winter storms in its face. Grace withereth without adversity.
The devil is but God's master fencer to teach us to handle
weapons!" And, in our time, Jonathan Chao of Hong Kong,
writing of the "suffering Church", says:

> The Church in China has been transformed from a timid,
> "foreign-coloured", institutional church into a bold, in-
> digenous, institutionless church, and it has been changed
> from a dependent "mission church" into an independent
> "missionary church". It is a Church that has gone through
> the "steps of the Cross", following the footsteps of her
> Lord: betrayal, trial, humiliation, abandonment, suffer-
> ing, death, burial, resurrection and the gift of the Spirit
> of Pentecost.

What, then, of the future? A stable government, in line
with Marxist theory on religion, is certainly committed to
implementing its policy of limited freedom; but even that
freedom would be endangered by further political turmoil.
In any case, no one need expect the door for Christianity to
open as wide as it was before 1949.

It is impossible to understand the situation in China
unless we see it as the sphere of a mighty conflict between
two kingdoms: the Kingdom of God and that of Satan. St.
Paul, in his Ephesian letter, described the cosmic conflict in
which the universal Church was locked in mortal combat
with the demonic powers opposed to Christ and His Kingdom. This is a global warfare in which the whole Body of
Christ is battling not primarily with earthly adversaries or
organisations – however hostile these may be – but with
the unseen world rulers of the present darkness and the
spiritual armies of wickedness in heavenly places. The
Enemy himself, the Prince of the power of the air, knowing
that his time is short, is deploying all his subtleties and wiles
to deceive, if possible, the very elect and so to win the

final victory. All Christians concerned about China and the Church in that land need to clothe themselves with the armour of God and exercise their God-given authority in prayer. As Watchman Nee has written: "It is the prayer ministry of the Church that causes action in Heaven. The manifestation of God's power may not exceed the prayer of the Church. Today the greatness of God's power is circumscribed by the extent of the Church's prayer." Then, surely, the time has come for the Church at prayer to release God's limitless power in China where a billion souls still wait to hear that Jesus Christ is Lord.

Nowhere in the world today does the Church need to be aware of the nature of the spiritual conflict so much as in China, where God is greatly multiplying His Church, but where Satan is massing his opposition. Alexander Solzhenitsyn, having lived in a society inspired solely by materialism and based on the explicit denial of the rights of the individual, says that "Where the state is sovereign, there can be no place for any other religion!" In China, as in Russia, the State is totally committed to abolishing religion, and the methods of achieving this end are both subtle and satanic.

But the Church in China is not doomed to destruction, for by His Cross and Resurrection Christ has conquered Satan: he is, even now, a defeated foe. May God open the eyes of all Chinese Christians to the spiritual realities of their situation! In the immediate future, however, the prospect is for intensified warfare which demands that the whole Body of Christ come to the aid of her hard-pressed brethren. Even though the principalities and powers will never cease their opposition to the Church of Jesus Christ, God has declared: "I will work and who will prevent Me?"

One thing is certain: the sheer power and momentum of the present movement of God's Spirit in China are beyond the power of man to halt. No one can foresee the political and social changes which may take place during the next decade, what direction the Church will take or what persecution it may endure, but one thing is sure – that the risen Lord according to His promise will not cease to build His

Church: "I will build My Church and the gates of hell shall not prevail against it!"

The day must surely come when China's martyr Church will bear her glorious witness, not only to her own people but to the whole world. Meanwhile, as God pours out His Spirit on His people, that Church, matured through suffering, is playing her part in the harvest of the last time.

> The Lord is King! lift up your voice,
> O earth, and all ye heavens, rejoice!
> From world to world the joy shall ring,
> The Lord omnipotent is King!
>
> The Lord is King! who then shall dare
> Resist His will, distrust His care,
> Or murmur at His wise decrees,
> Or doubt His royal promises?
>
> The Lord is King! child of the dust,
> The Judge of all the earth is just;
> Holy and true are all His ways;
> Let every creature speak His praise.
>
> He reigns! ye saints, exalt your strains;
> Your God is King, your Father reigns;
> And He is at the Father's side,
> The Man of love, the Crucified.
>
> One Lord, one empire, all secures;
> He reigns, and life and death are yours;
> Through earth and heaven one song shall ring,
> The Lord omnipotent is King!

Josiah Conder

Appendix: (Hong Kong)

Hong Kong is, without question, an integral part of China. The cession of the island to Britain by the terms of the Treaty of Nanking, which compelled China to legalise the opium trade with British India, is one of the most shameful chapters in British history. Subsequently Kowloon and the New Territories were added to constitute the colony as it now is. That the Treaties of Nanking and Tientsin were unjust it would be hard to deny, and China has every right to look forward to resuming sovereignty over the whole territory in 1997. Britain should concede that right immediately.

But Hong Kong today is not the barren rock and pirate lair it was in 1842. Wise British rule over the territory for over 160 years has afforded the opportunity for the unique commercial skills of the Chinese to create a truly beautiful and wonderfully prosperous free port with a population of nearly five million people. Trading vessels of all nations are always at anchor in Hong Kong's magnificent harbour. Industry flourishes, and the splendid high-rise buildings in the city centre of Victoria and in Kowloon and the luxury homes of both Chinese and Europeans are evidences of the wealth which the colony has accumulated. The fine university and many splendid hospitals are a credit to the administration. Hong Kong's development never ceases, the latest achievements being the road tunnel beneath the strait connecting the island with Kowloon, the new complex of roads, underpasses and flyovers and the ultra-modern air terminal. There is only one serious drawback: Hong Kong is indefensible, as was demonstrated in the last war, when Japan overran the colony in a matter of days. For one thing, it depends on China for much of its water and a lot of its essential food supplies.

The Christian Church moved in at an early date. The Anglicans established their own diocese and built their cathedral. Mission schools multiplied. Other churches were added until now in 1984 there are over 600 congregations representing a variety of denominational and non-denominational church groups. The largest denomination is the Church of Christ in China, a part of the church of that name which existed in China before 1949. While Christians total only about 14% of the population, their influence in the colony is considerable: Hong Kong is one of the most important centres strategically for the gospel in Asia. There are over twenty seminaries and Bible schools, and the interdenominational Graduate School of Theology opened in 1975. A number of missions and church organisations have set up offices there, including the Far East Broadcasting Company, in addition to several publishing houses which see China as their principal objective.

Recently capitalist Hong Kong has been suffering from shock and nerves at the thought of being taken over by China's Communist government in 1997, even though China has promised to make that place a special autonomous region and to allow the present economic system to remain unchanged for fifty years. Nevertheless there is much unrest and a serious threat to law and order, any increase in which could give China an excuse for early intervention.

Hong Kong has always been a very important asset to China's trade and banking, and the People's Republic does not intend to do anything to disturb the present Crown Colony's stability or to reduce her prosperity, on which her own depends. However, many wealthy Chinese and business tycoons are leaving the place, or making plans to do so, and Jardine and Matheson have transferred their head office to Bermuda. As the negotiations between Britain and China have dragged on, confidence in the future has fluctuated and stocks and shares dropped sharply with a consequent flight of capital. The satisfactory agreement now reached between Britain and China should ensure Hong Kong's continued peace and prosperity in the immediate future.

If the world of business and trade have faced an uncertain future, so also have the churches. The flood of refugees from the oppression and hardships under Communism has made Hong Kong residents aware of prevailing conditions in China, and they have no wish to exchange their own liberties and standards of living for those conditions. Christians are especially fearful. Although China's spokesman has said that religious freedom would remain unchanged after 1997, the Three-Self Patriotic Movement, with its bad track record, is already involving itself with the Christian Council in Hong Kong. Rumours say that the World Council of Churches has advised churches to cut down on such activities as Bible classes and youth work; indeed, the TSPM will certainly extend its authority to Hong Kong after 1997, if not before. Among those familiar with the activities of the TSPM in China there is a growing division: some are prepared to work with it; while others are strongly opposed, valuing the freedom of worship, opinion and assembly sadly lacking in China. China has promised non-interference with Christian institutions such as the social welfare and educational programmes. Church schools, which are responsible for 60% of grade school education, would be allowed to continue; even foreign personnel working with church organisations would not be excluded, it is said. Yet the fear remains. Should Christians and Christian agencies, like the business tycoons, prepare to leave? To this question there is no simple answer. Obviously a Communist authority would not permit the continuance of the activities of the FEBC to which the TSPM has been strongly opposed, but the closing of local studios would not affect Christian broadcasting to China. There must be doubt about the possibility of Christian publishers continuing their work without considerable censorship and it is impossible to foresee whether Christian literature, including Bibles, would be able to move "within China" more freely or not. Some organisations would be well advised to move elsewhere, but there need be no panicky large-scale exodus; rather, missions and churches should prepare themselves for whatever the future holds.

Clearly, the churches of Hong Kong can and should learn lessons from those of China. They should hasten to achieve total autonomy and independence of foreign control and financial support. They should encourage the growth of family gatherings or house groups within the framework of normal church life. A literature programme to complement the family group programme could be prepared. The churches must prepare their members to defend the faith against atheistic materialism by a study of Communism and Christianity. As a "middle-class" Church, the Church should reach out to Hong Kong's working classes, who can also be included in intensified lay leadership training schemes. But most important of all, the churches of Hong Kong should be taught to view the prospect of Hong Kong's assimilation into China as a golden and God-given opportunity to unite with the battle-hardened churches of China in the great task of evangelisation.

No one can be sure what kind of government will be in power in China in 1997 or what the Pacific and world situation will be in fourteen years' time. Perhaps the promises of today will not be fulfilled tomorrow, but the promises of God are sure, and His command to take no anxious thought about the future is valid whatever changes may lie ahead. Sufficient unto the day is the evil thereof! Certainly, the Church in Hong Kong has a mission in relation to China. In fulfilling that mission, courage will be needed to face whatever suffering and trials the coming changes may bring.

Notes

Chapter 3
1 Lyall, L., *Flame for God: John Sung*, Overseas Missionary Fellowship, 1954.

Chapter 5
1 Glover, A., *A Thousand Miles of Miracle*, CIM, 1905.

Chapter 12
1 Thompson, Phyllis, *The Reluctant Exodus*, Hodder & Stoughton, 1979.

Chapter 13
1 Hensman, P. R., *Yellow Peril or Red Hope?*, SCM Press, 1968.

Chapter 14
1 *God Still Lives in China*, China Bible Fund, 1974.

Chapter 15
1 Fung, Raymond, *Households of God*, World Council of Churches, 1982.
2 *Evangelism in China*, China Project Bulletin No. 23.

Chapter 18
1 Lyall, L., *New Spring in China*, Hodder & Stoughton, 1979.
2 Lyall, L., *Come Wind, Come Weather*, Hodder & Stoughton, 1960.